FOOD AT THE TIME OF THE BIBLE
OF THE

From Adam's Apple
To The Last Supper

BIBLE

Contents

Foreword

Biblical history virtually begins with an act of eating: Adam's and Eve's tastes of the forbidden fruit in the Garden of Eden. And throughout the Bible, food continues to play an essential role.

The act of eating was often much more than a matter of nourishing the body; it was imbued with sanctity. This might be difficult to imagine sometimes, especially if, like Abraham who "hurried" and "ran" to feed his angelic visitors (Gen. 18:6-7) you find yourself rushing to put the finishing touches on some all-important feast or just to get supper on the table on time!

But a restful pause over the pot might help bring to mind some memorable scriptural meals: At Mount Sinai for example, Moses and the elders dined together to seal their covenant with God (Ex. 24:11). Jacob and his father-in law Laban also shared a meal to seal a pact. (Gen. 31:54). And of course, the Last Supper, perhaps the best-remembered biblical meal of all time, was rich in covenant significance that made its elements fundamental to Christian theology and practice.

Offering a meal as part of a pact sometimes had dire consequences in the Bible. A certain "stew of red lentils", (Gen. 25:30) was served by Jacob to his brother Esau in sealing the transfer of Esau's birthright. The stew is best known in the King James Version as pottage, the selling of which has become a metaphor to describe giving away something valuable in exchange for very little.

Food was indeed a mover and a shaker of biblical history, as the story of Joseph and his brothers teaches us. Because the rain-watered Land of Israel could be fickle in its productiveness, its people looked to Egypt, where the Nile never failed to flood, as their breadbasket. And so, in a famine year in Canaan, the sons of Jacob migrated to the Land of the Pharaohs, where they found their long-lost brother Joseph, now the Pharaoh's Vizier. Here the brothers and their extended families grew and flourished until eventually the Pharaoh who knew not Joseph enslaved them. Later, the people that had meanwhile become the Children of Israel left Egypt under the leadership of Moses in the Exodus, one of the greatest liberation stories of all mankind. And it all started because food was not available in a certain year in Canaan!

Through a deeper look within the pages of this book at all the fascinating and surprising ways in which food and Scripture are linked, you will discover that the Bible, the inspiration of our spiritual lives, can be an inspiration in our kitchens and dining rooms as well. You will learn to cook and bake delicious dishes using the same ingredients our biblical ancestors did. Many of the recipes which we have selected are unique in culinary terms: they come directly from the Bible, or from the Mishna and Talmud (also known as the Oral Law, a collection of commentaries on the Bible first set down in writing in the early centuries after Jesus), which are authentic voices from the time of Jesus.

Research by scholars at the Neot Kedumim Biblical Landscape Reserve has enabled a comparison of the recipes of Roman food expert Apicius with a wide variety of dishes mentioned in the Bible, the Mishna, and the Talmud. At Neot Kedumim they have come up with recipes, some rich in calories, many richly spiced, but all rich in biblical significance, which you can reproduce in your own kitchen. You will be able to serve dishes to family and friends that our biblical ancestors enjoyed, from the tent of Abraham to the Last Supper, from a sumptuous royal serving to simple farmer's fare.

Enjoy everything to the fullest always remembering, of course, that man does not live by bread alone (Deut. 8:3, Matt. 4:4, Luke 4:4).

The Holy Land
The Land of Plenty

Pomegranates
from the hills of Galilee & Samaria

Figs
from the hills of Samaria

Fish
from the Sea of Galilee
& Mediterranean Sea

Dates
from Jericho

Wheat
from the southern plains

Galilee

The Sea of Galilee

Mediterranean Sea

Samaria

River Jordan

Costal Plain

Jericho

Jerusalem

Bethlehem

Judea

Dead Sea

Southern Plains

Olives
from the hills of Galilee, Ju
& Samaria

Melon
from the Coastal Plain

Grapes
from the southern plain
& Judean hills

Milk & Cheese
from the slopes of the Jude

Salt
from the Dead Sea

From the Garden of Eden to Gardens Everywhere
Culinary History and the Bible

In the Garden

Food, Genesis 2:9 tells us, is God's gift to humankind. Human life is certainly impossible for long without it. But food is more than mere sustenance. It plays an important role in all civilizations, with some of the most fascinating differences among cultures measured in terms of the availability and variety of food, how it is prepared, and even how it is eaten.

An ancient olive tree in the Garden of Gethsemane.

A Tilling Tale

The Bible tells us that the first tiller of the soil was Cain (Gen. 4:2). Cain was part of the generation that had realized that they could raise their crops in a permanent location, rather than moving from place to place to harvest whatever they happened to find growing there. People also learned how to irrigate that land. It took a great deal of work to bring water to the fields, "watering it by foot", as Deuteronomy 11:10 puts it, but the reward was tremendous proliferation in food variety.

As better agricultural tools evolved, people began to gather in more crops than they could eat. Desert-dwellers brought milk and cheese from their flocks to the villages, trade in surpluses evolved along new highways and byways, and cities developed at the important junctions. We can easily see that from the first grain that sprouted from the soil to the development of international trade routes, the production and processing of food fundamentally changed human community life.

The Holy Land: The Right Place at the Right Time

The first place on earth to witness the entire process, from tillers and herdsmen to city-dwelling traders and food producers, was the Holy Land. The Holy Land is located in the Fertile Crescent, a region that arches over the deserts of what is now eastern Jordan, Iraq, and Iran and Saudi Arabia. On the northeastern end of the Crescent is Mesopotamia, once home to several biblical kingdoms. Mesopotamia, watered by the Tigris and the Euphrates rivers, was fertile land, and a major regional source of barley, sesame and linseed oil, flax, wheat, and sheeps' wool and goats' hair. Southern Mesopotamia specialized in dates and in fish.

Plowing the rocky soil in age-old fashion.

At the other end of the Crescent, in the southeast, was Egypt with its water source, the Nile. The vegetables and other food produced in the Kingdom of the Nile were

An ancient water wheel

famous "...We remember the fish we ate in Egypt at no cost; also the cucumbers, melons, leeks, onions and garlic" (Num. 11:5). Israelites also recalled the meat of which they were deprived in their wanderings (Num. 11:4). Thus the phrase "the fleshpots of Egypt" came to mean "ultimate plenty."

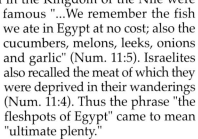

The shadoof is an ancient method of irrigation still in use in Egypt. A pole on a pivot holds a bucket at one end, balanced by a clay counterweight at the other end, thereby minimizing the labor of lifting water from the river to canals or into the fields.

The route of choice between these two extremities of the Fertile Crescent passed, via the "highway from Egypt to Assyria" (Is. 19:23), directly through the Holy Land. It was to be the key to much biblical history and it can be said that the fate of the kingdoms of Israel and Judah was decided by it.

On the Biblical Table

"Milk and honey" were both among the earliest foods of humankind and the earliest foods mentioned in the Bible. One explanation for the famous phrase describing the Holy Land, "a land flowing with milk and honey" (Exod. 3:8 and Deut. 26:15), is that it describes grazing land, one that is not permanently or intensely cultivated (Isa. 7:21-24), land that also sprouts the wildflowers from

This aerial view of the Nile River dramatically demonstrates its green, life-giving course through the desert.

Luscious pomegranates ready for harvest.

which bees produce honey. The archaeologists tell us that when the Israelites first came into the mountainous areas of the Holy Land, this was the kind of land they found, and there they built the first permanent dwellings. Eventually, they began to raise grain during the winter rainy season, and grapes, olives, figs, and other fruits in the dry summer months (Deut. 11:4). The growing list of produce of the land of Israel, known as the "Seven Species" (Deut. 8:8), included wheat, barley, grapes, figs, olives, pomegranates, and dates.

Later, the typical list of staples that Jesse sent with his son David to re-supply his other sons fighting the Philistines with King Saul (with an extra treat for the man in charge) included grain and milk products. "Take this ephah of roasted grain and these ten loaves of bread for your brothers," Jesse instructed David, "and hurry to their camp. Take along these ten cheeses to the commander of their unit" (1 Sam. 17:17-18).

To smooth things over after her husband Nabal insulted David, Abigail also chose that well-known and very effective element of conflict-resolution: food. 1 Samuel 25:18 says, "Abigail lost no time. She took two hundred loaves of bread, two skins of wine, five dressed sheep,

Detail of the ancient Sepphoris synagogue mosaic: Baskets of First Fruits for offering in the Temple.

five seahs of roasted grain, a hundred cakes of raisins and two hundred cakes of pressed figs, and loaded them on donkeys." We notice that Abigail went all out with her diplomatic efforts: among the food that Abigail gave David was meat, a delicacy usually reserved for special occasions.

Ezekiel (4:9) was commanded by God to mix "beans and lentils, millet and spelt" [a kind of wheat which he was to bake into what today's natural foods aficionados would call "multi-grain bread"], while Isaiah (28:25) adds spice to the list (literally): "Does he not sow caraway and scatter cummin?" Matthew (23:23) knew cummin as a spice valuable enough to levy a tariff on it, as well as on mint and anise.

Food for Body and Soul: The Main Bible Festivals

Pilgrimage to Jerusalem, by Oleg Trabish.

Although the various biblical festivals are essentially spiritual occasions, in their earliest form they were agricultural festivals that centered on the need of human beings to ensure the success of their crops by entreating God's intervention. During the 50-day period between Passover and the Feast of Weeks, each day was counted as the farmer worriedly surveyed his field. Most of the rainy season had passed and an unseasonable downpour just as the grain was ripening on the stalks could destroy the crop (Exod. 9:31). So could an unseasonable heat wave. In Jewish tradition, certain rituals of mourning attached themselves to this period known as the "counting of the Omer," an Omer being a sheaf of wheat. It was almost as if people were afraid to be "too happy" lest the promise of the season end in disaster due to the changeable weather at this time of year.

In the days of Jesus, the readiness of certain crops for harvest actually determined the calendar itself. Anyone born on February 29th can tell you that in the present-day secular calendar of the western world, a legacy of the Romans, a day is added at the end of February every four years by convention. But in ancient times, it was the

Biblical Agricultural Year

*"While the earth remains,
Seedtime and harvest
And cold and heat
And summer and winter"
(Num. 3:23)*

WINTER
*"We remember
the...leeks and the
onions and
garlic"
(Num. 11:5)*

SPRING
*"They came
to Bethlehem
at the beginning
of the barley harvest.
(Ruth 1:22)*

AUTUMN
*... a cake of
dates...
of raisins"
(2 Sam. 6:19)*

SUMMER
*"Now in the days
of wheat harvest...
(Gen. 30:14)
"grapes...with some
of the pomegranates
and the figs"
(Num. 3:23)*

*"This month shall be the beginning
of months for you" (Ex.12:2)*

The Gezer Calendar, carved on limestone in the tenth century BCE, and possibly a student's writing exercise (one of the earliest Hebrew inscriptions ever discovered) gives us a good description of harvest seasons in Israel in the 10th century BCE. The Gezer Calendar is a rhythmic enumeration of the agricultural seasons, something similar to "thirty days hath September... "

Two months are vine pruning: (July-August)
Two months are harvest (August-September: Figs and Grapes)
Two months are planting: (October-November: Grain)
Two months are late: (December-January) [planting] February
One month is hoeing flax: (March)
One month is barley harvest (April)
One month is harvest and feasting (May-June)

expected availability of the harvest that determined the Jewish calendar: if the holiday of Passover, which celebrates the barley harvest, was just around the calendrial corner, and it appeared upon examination by experts that the grain would not be ripe (or the calves or doves of a proper size for sacrifice) another lunar month, a "leap-month", would be added to the calendar so that all elements necessary for celebration would be ready.

The Biblical Dietary Do's and Don'ts

Customs associated with raising and consuming food are pillars of many of the world's religious beliefs, and faith plays an important role in determining what foods can go on the table. This is certainly true of the faith of the Bible. One of the ways of marking the difference between the Israelites and the surrounding cultures was simply to do things differently when it came to food and food cultivation. For example, during the Feast of Tabernacles, the Israelites were required to "live in booths for seven days" (Lev. 23:42). In Canaan, the Israelites found that people lived in booths in their orchards and

A map of the ancient Near East showing the routes by which food and other goods traveled back and forth between distant kingdoms.

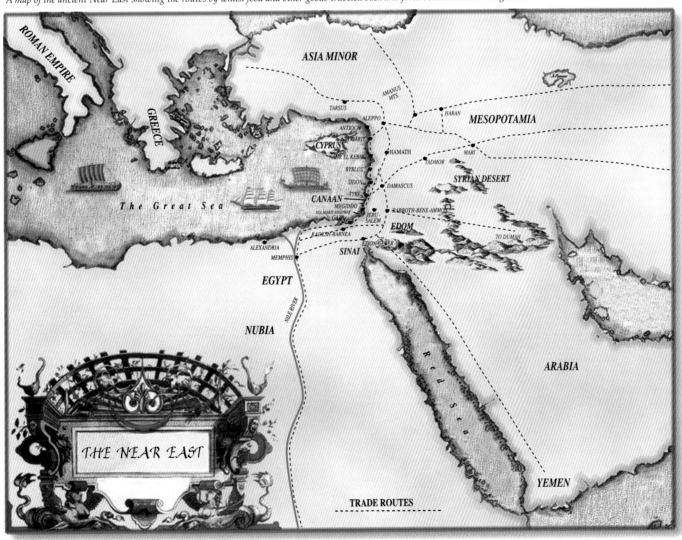

ROMAN EMPIRE

ASIA MINOR

AMANUS MTS.

TARSUS
ALEPPO
HARAN
MESOPOTAMIA

GREECE

ANTIOCH
UGARIT
CYPRUS
NAHR EL KEBIR
HAMATH
MARI
TADMOR

BYBLOS
SIDON
TYRE
DAMASCUS
SYRIAN DESERT

The Great Sea

CANAAN
MEGIDDO
VIA MARIS HIGHWAY
GAZA
JERU-SALEM
RABBOTH-BENE-AMMON

KADESH-BARNEA
EDOM
TO DUMAH

ALEXANDRIA
EZION-GEBER
MEMPHIS
SINAI

EGYPT

NILE RIVER

NUBIA

Red Sea

ARABIA

THE NEAR EAST

YEMEN

TRADE ROUTES

Detail of the ancient Tiberias synagogue mosaic: summer fruits personified as a woman holding a cluster of grapes.

reptiles, and birds. Then I heard a voice telling me, 'Get up, Peter. Kill and eat'. I replied, 'Surely not, Lord! Nothing impure or unclean has ever entered my mouth. 'The voice spoke from heaven a second time, 'Do not call anything impure that God has made clean'" (Acts 11:5-9).

Medieval Jewish philosopher Maimonides, who was also a physician, believed that there were valid health reasons to avoid eating certain animals. The pig, Maimonides said, was "very dirty and feeds on dirty things..." and "...blood is difficult to digest..." About a century later, another famed commentator, Nahmanides, looked similarly at fish. "The reason for specifying fins and scales is that fish which have fins and scales get closer to the surface of the water... those without fins and scales usually live in the lower muddy strata and... musty swamps and eating them can be injurious to the health."

The other well-known Jewish dietary law, the separation between milk and meat, derives from Exodus 23:19, 34:26, and Deuteronomy 14:21 which prohibit boiling a young goat in its mother's milk. Scholars have suggested that this prohibition may derive from a sense of respect for the mother-offspring bond; or it may have been to avoid an act that was carried out by other peoples in Canaan as part of a pagan rite.

vineyards at the height of summer, in order to personally guard the ripening fruit, and after the fall harvest they moved back to their homes. Thus, the Israelites emphasized the difference between themselves and their faith in the One God, and the surrounding Canaanite culture by moving into booths precisely when everyone else was moving inside!

Leviticus 11 and Deuteronomy 14:3-21 provide lists of animals, dividing them between the "clean" and "unclean" food. That which was clean was "fit" for consumption, the meaning of the Hebrew word "kosher". One of the best-known biblical food prohibitions in this realm is against pork. This prohibition was so strict that archaeologists can determine which ancient settlements were inhabited by Israelites according to the absence of pig bones in their excavations. For example, on Mount Ebal in Samaria, archaeologists discovered an altar dating from the period deemed to be immediately after the Israelite conquest. Among the bones discovered near the altar were only animals on the "clean" list, including cattle, sheep, goats, and deer.

Animals from the "forbidden list" appear as a metaphor in Peter's vision on the rooftop of Simon the Tanner, where he sees "...something like a large sheet being let down from heaven by its four corners... I looked into it and saw four-footed animals of the earth, wild beasts,

The idea of separating different classes of things has other aspects, too, among them the idea that to be "holy" is to some extent to be "separate". The holiness which God required of the Israelites (Exod. 22:30, Lev. 11:44-45 inter alia) mandated separating themselves from a class of items considered unclean, and separating various classes of items from each other. From Bible days, "separation" also meant not consuming the food of gentiles because it might have been intended for use in idol-worshipping ceremonies (Zech. 9:6-7; Ezra 9:1).

Roman-era Jewish philosopher Philo saw a symbolic meaning in the permission granted by God to eat certain foods and to refrain from eating other kinds. People increased in wisdom only if they had to consider carefully all aspects of life that would lead them to be more moral by "chewing them over." A way of remembering to do this would be to only eat those animals that chew their cud!

An ancient Egyptian tomb mural showing the deceased with his wife, dressed in festive clothing and performing agricultural chores. The deceased plows while his wife sows; he then reaps with a sickle while she walks behind to gather the stalks.

In seeking ways to explain biblical commandments to refrain from eating certain animals and from consuming blood, some have revived an idea of the ancient Church father Theophilus, who said, "There were no carnivorous animals before Adam's fall." They look at the fact that God's plan, according to Genesis 1:29, was that mankind eat only fruit and vegetables. After the flood, a concession was made to human frailty, and animals were also permitted to be eaten (Gen. 9:3). But self-control would still have to be exercised. One way to do this was to determine that blood, the life force, was not to be consumed under any circumstances (Lev. 17:13-14 inter alia). This prohibition is virtually unknown among any other ancient people.

Today's thinkers continue to delve more deeply into the meaning for Jewish dietary restrictions. For example, they are seen as a means of "negotiating" between that which is spiritual and that which is physical, with an understanding that extremes of appetite are not limited to the intake of food. Could not discipline of the physical appetite reduce the craving for acquisitiveness, and even increase "spiritual hunger" for justice and compassion?

A Taste of Heaven: Meal as Metaphor

Food has given us one of the most powerful and enduring of spiritual symbols. From the first Passover to the Last Supper, certain foods, notable among them wine and bread, have become deeply ingrained in sacred memory for both Jews and Christians. Bread, leavened and unleavened, grapes and wine, salt, leavening, the sowing of seed, all appear in scriptural lessons, and the meal

Ripe dates hang heavy on the tree.

itself had symbolic aspects, among them welcoming guests, like Abraham, or ending hostilities, as Isaac did after negotiating with Abimelech over ownership of the wells at Beersheba, when he "made them a feast, and they ate and drank" (Gen. 26:30). To this day in the Middle East, the "breaking of bread" with one's former enemy is an important symbol of the end of hostilities. This is one interpretation attached to the famous words of Psalm 23:5: "You prepare a table before me in the presence of my enemies".

The Bible used the basic physical activity of eating to help us better relate to elements from the world of ideas. Says Proverbs 9:1-6: "Wisdom has prepared her meat and mixed her wine; she has also set her table. She has sent out her maids, and she calls from the highest point of the city. 'Let all who are simple come in here!' she says to those who lack judgment. 'Come, eat my food and drink the wine I have mixed. Leave your simple ways and you will live; walk in the way of understanding'". In these verses, Wisdom is engaging in simple domestic tasks, like the singer in the Song of Songs 8:2, or the men of Isaiah 5:22. Preparing a table was as common then as now, as is mentioned in Isaiah 21:5 and Psalm 78:19, as well as in 2 Kings 4:10. Wisdom is hosting a banquet that brings life, as does God in Psalm 23:5, and Isaiah 25:6.

The New Testament emphasizes the "cross-over" of water from the physical to the spiritual. In John 4:13-14, the story of the encounter with the Samaritan woman, Jesus says of well water, "Everyone who drinks this water will be thirsty again, but whoever drinks the water I give him will never thirst. Indeed, the water I give him will become in him a spring of water welling up to eternal life." The giving of spiritual life in terms of food is also reflected in the Eucharist food and wine that gives life, or, as Church father Hippolytus put it," ...the spiritual divine table."

It is the wonderful world of metaphor and symbolism that allows us to link our spiritual lives to that which we eat, and find value far beyond the culinary in all we learn about the biblical history of food.

Drawing water from a well using a traditional pulley system.

	Milestones in the Bible & Region	Milestones in the Food Production
Pre-Pottery Neolithic	*Biblical city in existence at this time: Jericho, the oldest city in the world*	
Pottery Neolithic 6000 - 4300.	*Biblical city founded at this time: Beit Shean*	- The invention of pottery enables people to produce portable containers. - Economy based on agriculture and the beginnings of cattle breeding. - Sickle blades, chisels, axes, and knives discovered at the world's oldest city, Jericho.
Chalcolithic 4300-3300 BCE	*Biblical cities founded at this time: Beer Sheva, Gezer, Arad.*	- Floodwaters made available for irrigation and drinking by digging shallow pits in the desert riverbeds near Beersheba. - The first date pits discovered in Ein Gedi by the Dead Sea. Also: Wheat, barley, olives, garlic, onion, pomegranates, lentils, and nuts. - Presence of olives indicates trade. - Intense palm tree cultivation begins at this time. - The Golan Heights economy is based on herding - Olive trees grown for the first time, and olive oil first produced, probably in the Golan Heights. - Most pottery vessels handmade, but the first small vessels produced on a potter's wheel appear at this time. - The flint industry expands; the first stone axes for turning the soil appear, and sickle blades for harvesting. - Large pottery containers, the pithoi, a sign of settled people. - The first cheese-making appears.
Early Bronze I 3300-3040 BCE	*Biblical cities founded at this time: Hazor; Megiddo.*	- New crops introduced into the mountain areas, grapes and figs. - Bottle gourd seeds first found in Egyptian tombs.
Early Bronze II-III 3050-2300 BCE	*Biblical city founded at this time: Ai.*	- Cities emerge, with complex systems of government, administration, and social hierarchies. - At Arad in the Negev, barley, wheat and legumes (peas, lentils and chickpeas) were found. Grapes and olives become major hill country crops. Oil and wine intended for trade with the cities of the plains, where grain was the major crop, and with semi-nomadic pastoralists who supplied meat and skins. - Stone-lined storage pits appear in Arad. - The animal-drawn plow appears for the first time, replacing the older hoeing stick. - The water reservoir of the city of Ai, which could contain some 5 million gallons of surface runoff, was built. - A log serving as a beehive is the earliest evidence of domesticated honey production.
Early Bronze IV Middle Bronze I 2300-2000	*Beginning of the Period of the Patriarchs.*	- An interim period following the collapse of the urban culture of the previous period (due to climate and social factors, as well as invasions from Egypt). - The economy of the small cities that survived this crisis depended on agriculture and herding.
Middle Bronze IIA 2000-1800/1750 BCE	*The Amorites (Gen. 10:16) can first be traced to Mesopotamia at this time.*	- A clay vessel serving as a beehive discovered in Egypt, dating from 1900 BCE.
Middle Bronze II B-C1800/1750-1550	*The first written documents appear, in the cuneiform Akkadian language.*	
Late Bronze I 1550-1400	*Israelites are enslaved in Egypt. The Hittites (Gen. 23:10, inter alia) establish their empire. The international marine trade is established, along with several cities on the coast.*	- Small agricultural communities disappear, perhaps followed by an increase in herding. - First pottery imported from Cyprus at this time; not a size that could be used as a container, therefore probably considered fine tableware. Mycenaean pottery from Greece also imported for this reason. - Egypt imports wine from Canaan. - Egypt imports carobs from Canaan.
Late Bronze II A-B 1400-1200	*First mention of "Hebrews" in the Land of Israel in an Egyptian stele dating from 1220 BCE.*	

Iron IA 1200-1150	*Israelite settlement emerges, apparently first in the central hill country, Transjordan, and the northern Negev and later in the Galilee.* *The arrival of the Philistines and other Sea Peoples from the islands of the eastern Mediterranean (Amos 9:7).*	- Large open spaces in the villages probably served as livestock paddocks and grain storage. - Herding an important part of the economy at this time. - Increased construction of plastered cisterns allow water storage for increased agriculture. - Large pottery pithoi discovered at these sites may have been used for water. - Storage pits and silos dug into the ground may have served to hold crops. - Economy of these places based on barter with inhabitants of hill country that specialized in horticulture and herding. - Construction of terraces for agriculture, reflected in the Biblical injunction to "clear the land" (Josh 17:15).
Iron IB 1150-1000	*Period of the Judges*	
Iron IIA 1000-925	*The United Monarchy: Solomon's central store cities grow; surrounding villages economically dependent on them.*	- Settlement increases in the Negev near springs; water was collected in large, open reservoirs. - The Gezer agricultural calendar a tenth-century BCE "farmer's almanac"dates from this period.
Iron II B925-720	*The Divided Monarchy. Lachish conquered by the Assyrians (721 BCE).*	- Large public storage facilities and granaries show that Hazor was a central food repository at this time. - Jerusalem expanded to about 150 acres, supported by villages and farms in the periphery. - fortified, agricultural villages. An increasing number of farmsteads - known in the bible as literally "daughters of..." major towns (Josh 15:47, Josh 17:11, inter alia,) established. - Conquest of Lachish shows grapevines. - The Greeks manufacture artificial hives.
Iron IIC 720-586	*Arad destroyed, probably by the Edomites* *First Temple destroyed by the Babylonians: 586 BCE.*	- Extensive oil industry operated by the Philistines at Ekron - over one hundred oil presses. Presses found in ordinary houses, indicating that this was a cottage industry. - Wine production: presses found at Gibeon, settling basins, and fermentation tanks cit in the rock. 63 cisterns for storing wine in jars. (25,000 gallons!) - One of the Arad Ostraca (belonging to Elyashib, commander of the Arad fortress in its last phase (probably destroyed by the Edomites) "and now, give the Kittim (mercenaries in the Judean army, maybe from Cyprus) three baths of wine, and write the name of the day. And from the rest of the first flour, send one homer of flour in order to make bread for them. Give them the wine from the aganoth vessels." These supplies were sent from the southern Judean hills to Arad, and distributed from here.
Persian Period 586-332	*The return to Zion at the time of Cyrus the Great (553 BCE) (Ezra 1:1-2)*	- Development of agriculture in the Jordan Valley includes a sophisticated water system to channel water from mountain springs to the valley. - A large bowl called a mortarium, and not found outside the Land of Israel, which may have been used for processing cereal products, indicates the importance of such products.
Hellenistic Period 332-37	*Rome takes over the Holy Land towards the end of this period (63 BCE), replacing the Hasmoneans, descendants of Judah the Macabbee who had ruled for the previous 100 years.*	- The spice trade begins with the Nabateans, the forerunners of the Arabs, who ruled from their capital in Petra. - Increase import of Mediterranean fish to Holy Land cities.
Roman Period 37 BCE-324 CE	*The birth of Jesus, ca 6 BCE. Crucifixion of Jesus: ca 33 CE. The destruction of the Temple: 70 CE.* *Extensive trade on roads built by the Romans especially for this purpose. (Rev. 18:12).*	- Sugar cane first comes to the Holy Land - Cypriot wine imported to the Holy Land - The stone-weight press is replaced by the screw press for the manufacture of olive oil.

Dining Customs in Bible Days

"While they were reclining at the table eating..." (Mark 14:18)

The Hebrew Scriptures contain numerous references to meals, both simple and sumptuous. The Bible relates that when the Queen of Sheba - apparently no pauper herself according to the entourage she brought with her - saw the food on the king's table, "she was overwhelmed" (1 Kings 10:5). No wonder, for 1 Kings 4:22-23 tells us that, "Solomon's daily provisions were thirty cors of fine flour and sixty cors of meal, ten head of stall-fed cattle, twenty of pasture-fed cattle and a hundred sheep and goats, as well as deer, gazelles, roebucks and choice fowl."

The simplest meal in the Bible is perhaps the bread and water consumed by the "man of God from Judah" in 1 Kings 13:19.

Ruth the Moabitess in her traditional pose gleaning barley in the fields of Boaz. Drawing by Oleg Trabish

A simple peasant's meal is amply illustrated by the menu at the first "lunch date" of Ruth and Boaz, bread dipped in wine vinegar and toasted grain (Ruth 2:14), all of which could be easily transported to the fields and consumed on a break in the farmer's workday.

Throughout the Bible, life cycle events were a prime reason for a feast: In Genesis 21:8 Abraham holds a feast at Isaac's weaning. Laban gave a feast in honor of Jacob's marriage, to Leah as it turned out instead of Jacob's

beloved Rachel (Gen. 29:22). The wedding in Cana (John 2:1) was also a festive meal in celebration of a wedding (the actual ceremony may have taken place months before). The fact that a feast was customary at weddings is also noted in the story of Samson, where that burly bridegroom was the host (Judges 14:10). Samson's wedding feast lasted seven days, a custom that is reflected in the modern Jewish practice of reciting seven blessings at the wedding ceremony, and marked among traditional Jews to this day with 'feasts' in the homes of friends and relatives each day for six more days after the wedding.

Other kinds of public events were also accompanied by a festive meal, one unfortunate example being the story of the Golden Calf (Ex. 32:6): "So the next day the people rose early and sacrificed burnt offerings and presented fellowship offerings. Afterward they sat down to eat and drink and got up to indulge in revelry." At a feast held to mark the conclusion of the sheep shearing, the Bible records that Abigail found Nabal "holding a banquet like that of a king" (1 Sam. 25:36).

One Hebrew term for banquet, *mishteh,* from the root word 'drink', makes it clear that imbibing drinks, especially wine (Isa. 24:9), was customary - although Proverbs 23:21, as well as later rabbinic sources, warn repeatedly against the evils of drinking too much.

One of the most famous banquets in the Bible is described in the book of Esther, where "wine was served in goblets of gold, each different from the other..." (Esther 1:7). Men and women did not sit together at such banquets, as shown by

An isometric representation of the Herodian Mansion in Jerusalem's Jewish Quarter. The large room on the left could have served as a banquet hall.

the fact that Queen Vashti gave a feast of her own for the women. From Isaiah 5:12 we deduce that music, perhaps an ancient form of chamber music featuring several instruments, was a part of festive meals. The appearance of Queen Vashti demanded by her husband may also have been expected as entertainment.

Breaking Bread Together

We can see in some Bible stories that which we know to be true in our daily lives: the manner in which food is served and consumed spoke volumes about the nature of the relationships at the table and beyond. Abraham,

Ancient vessels discovered in excavations in Jerash, Jordan

for example, "hurried" to serve the messenger/angels that came to him (Gen. 18:6). The alacrity with which Abraham responded to the needs of his guests was forever to link the characteristic of warm hospitality to the Patriarch and to his descendants. Isaac shared a grand meal with that old family rival Abimelech as a sign of reconciliation after their quarrel over use of the well at what became Beersheba (Gen. 26:30). Once a meal was shared, it was a sign that peace had come between the diners. To this day among the desert-dwelling Bedouin (many of whose customs can be traced to the Bible), the serving of a meal within one's tent is synonymous with the extending of protection.

Food continued to be a prime means of showing hospitality, as we can see in Luke 10:8: "When you enter a town and are welcomed, eat what is set before you".

The presence of a guest under one's roof was considered literally a God-given opportunity to do a good deed. This was especially emphasized after the destruction of the Second Jerusalem Temple, when the sages sought to provide people with substitutes for the Temple sacrifices considered so essential in the worship of God. It was important to "prolong the meal at the table", it was said, but not just to socialize. The reason was rather

"because a poor man may come along and the host will give him something to eat". One ancient homily encourages this behavior by drawing an otherwise not-so-obvious connection between Exodus 27:1 "the altar of wood three cubits high" and Ezekiel 41:22, "This is the table that is before the Lord". "Why does the verse begin by calling it an altar and end by calling it a table? Because ... as long as the Temple stood, the altar made expiation for Israel, but now a man's table makes expiation for him."

The Jewish Sabbath and holiday table itself is considered a means of commemorating worship in the Temple, because it contains three elements featured in the Covenant-promise of God to the people, "grain, wine, and oil" (Deut. 11:14). Another custom adopted since the Middle Ages is the singing of hymns at Sabbath meals, as the Levites once sang Psalms in the Temple courts.

Fasting

The first specific mention of fasting in the Bible is as a means of showing remorse and invoking God's forgiveness, when David prayed for the life of Bathsheba's first child, which he had fathered (2 Sam. 12:16). The specific purpose of fasting, which may have been one method of "denying" oneself, as mentioned in Numbers 30:13, is noted in Ezra 8:21 "so that we might humble ourselves before God". Isaiah also notes that fasting was a means of humbling oneself before God (Isa. 58:3-4). However Isaiah and other prophets note that fasting is a means to an end, and to be effective must be accompanied by real repentance.

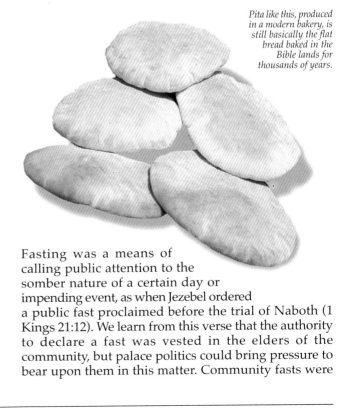

Pita like this, produced in a modern bakery, is still basically the flat bread baked in the Bible lands for thousands of years.

Fasting was a means of calling public attention to the somber nature of a certain day or impending event, as when Jezebel ordered a public fast proclaimed before the trial of Naboth (1 Kings 21:12). We learn from this verse that the authority to declare a fast was vested in the elders of the community, but palace politics could bring pressure to bear upon them in this matter. Community fasts were

Utensils and a table from the Roman era discovered in excavations in Jerusalem's Jewish Quarter.

The Order of the Meal

Today's host or hostess, taking pains over the hors d'oeuvres and setting out a beautifully presented platter in the living room while finishing preparations in the kitchen for the main meal, will appreciate the similarity of today's customs to the ancient order of the meal, as described in a minor tractate of the Jerusalem Talmud, *Derech Eretz Zuta*, which has its origins in the second century CE: "The guests enter the waiting room, and sit on benches or high backed chairs until all the guests have arrived". We see this same courtesy reflected in 1 Cor. 11:33-34 when Paul advises, "when you come together to eat, wait for each other."

At the next stage of the meal, states the above source, "a cup of wine is mixed for them, and each one says a blessing by himself. Then appetizers are brought, and each one says the blessing by himself. After that, they go up to the dining area and recline. Again water is brought to wash the hands ... another cup of wine is mixed for the guests ... another blessing is said, but now one guest says it for all the others."

Another custom in vogue in ancient Jerusalem, according to the Mishna, might be a boon to many a nervous modern day host waiting for a tardy guest while dinner burns to a crisp: "In Jerusalem there was the strict custom that, as long as napkins were draped over the door, guests might continue to enter. Once the napkins were removed, no more guests were permitted to enter."

At the Table

At the time of Jesus, among the Roman pagans, women and children did not eat their meal at the same table as men. However Jewish families rejected this custom, and had their meal together. Hollywood notwithstanding, we must not imagine all ancient people constantly dining at sumptuous feasts. Most of the world, then

also declared when calamity was at the door, such as when war threatened (Judg. 20:26; 1 Sam. 7:6; 2 Chron. 20:3; Jer. 36:3). The only fixed fast day in the Bible was Yom Kippur, the Day of Atonement (Lev. 16:29 - "the fast" of Acts 27:9). After the destruction of the First Temple, however, a number of fixed fast days came into being (Zech. 8:19).

Moses fasted for forty days (Ex. 34:28), as did Jesus (Matt. 4:2). Esther fasted for three days, and instructed the Jews of Susa to do the same, before her audience with King Ahasuerus (Esther 4:16). But for the most part, fasting was limited to 24 hours although the apocryphal Book of Judith 4:13 notes a fast that lasted for several days. Fasting was eventually prohibited on the Sabbath day and other festivals, in order not to mar the joy of the day.

In the days of Jesus, fasting was not uncommon (Luke 2:37; Luke 18:12; Mark 2:18). The Talmud notes that fasting was perceived as a means of atoning for sin or even of preventing sin. The Talmudic tractate *Nedarim* notes that it was common to fast on the anniversary of the death of a parent or a revered teacher. Fasting was accompanied by prayer, both public and private. Scholars point out that in other Near Eastern cultures, young children and even animals were required to fast. But in Jewish tradition, children, as well as pregnant and nursing mothers were exempt.

Jesus mandated certain behavior for the individual who was fasting which, according to Daniel 10:2-3 and 2 Samuel 12:16-20, and numerous references in the Talmud, seems to have been contrary to common practice. The fasting person was not to appear to be suffering, but was to "put oil on your head and wash your face, so that it will not be obvious to men that you are fasting, but only to your Father, who is unseen" (Matt. 6:16-17).

A typical wedding feast in the days of Jesus.

as now, did not do so; farmers for example would eat a light breakfast in the later hours of the morning (such as the one Ruth and Boaz shared) and have their main meal in the evening. Because hospitality was considered such an important aspect of life, guests were often invited to share a meal. On three occasions Luke notes that Jesus was a guest at the table of certain Pharisees (Luke 7:36; 11:38 14:1).

As noted, a poor man was more than welcome at the table, but custom mandated a specific seating order, extending even to who took his seat first. "At a session of study, precedence is to be given to wisdom; in reclining at a feast, to age." This custom seems to be one of the Bible's most ancient. It is also mentioned in the story of Joseph's reunion with his brothers. "The men had been seated before him in the order of their ages, from the firstborn to the youngest; When portions were served to them from Joseph's table, Benjamin's portion was five times as much as anyone else's. So they feasted and drank freely with him" (Gen. 43:33-34). Seniority in seating order might also be reflected in the disciples' argument "as to which of them would be accounted the greatest", which took place at the table at the end of the Last Supper (Luke 22:24).

Cups and vessels from Zippori (Sepphoris)

　　　The earliest meaning of the word "table" was a piece of leather or a mat, which was spread on the floor. By Jesus' day, tables were of various shapes. In the Greek New Testament, one type of table mentioned is a *trapeza*, indicating a four-sided table (Matt. 15:27, for example). But more often, the word *triclinium* is used, indicating that the diners were reclining at a three-sided table, about the height of today's coffee table and surrounded by low couches, that was common in the Roman world. Tables were made of wood or stone, and of two parts, the base and the dining surface. After a meal, the entire surface piece would be taken outside and "shaken" to remove food remnants, especially from the one-third of the table where the serving dishes would

be placed. The rest of the table would be covered with a tablecloth.

A serving table and dishes from the Herodian mansions in Jerusalem's Jewish Quarter.

Perhaps the most famous of the New Testament references to reclining at table is in the story of the Last Supper, the Passover meal, where "the disciple whom Jesus loved was reclining next to him" (John 13:23). Reclining became synonymous with dining, as the Babylonian Talmud notes: "the scrupulous among the people of Jerusalem would not go to a feast until they learned who was to recline with them". The custom of reclining, where a meal could be leisurely enjoyed, was perceived as the prerogative of free people. As such, it was practiced by all people at the Passover meal as another means of signifying freedom from slavery. Simple people did not take the time to recline at their meals as a rule, and slaves certainly did not. Around most Passover tables throughout the contemporary Jewish world, while actual reclining is not an option, the custom is alluded to by the presence of a pillow at the chair of the head of the table, the seat of the person who oversees the ceremonial aspects of the meal.

A bowl for the washing of hands would be proffered to each guest according to seniority. The washing of hands was primarily ceremonial (Mark 7:2-4) while the washing of feet, another ancient custom, was doubtless an aesthetic consideration. Washing of the feet is noted in the story of Abraham's welcoming of the angels (Gen. 18:4), in the Song of Songs 5:3, as well as when Jesus reclines at the table of Simon the Pharisee (Luke 7:36-38) and at the Last Supper (John 13:5). This custom came from the desert, where people would enter the tent with feet dusty from the outdoors. To this day, among the Bible lands' desert dwellers, the Bedouin, it is still the custom when seated in the tent to fold one's feet beneath or behind oneself rather than in sight of the person seated opposite.

The washing of the disciples' feet by Jesus, of course, takes on greater significance than merely the aesthetic. It has been noted by scholars that the last act anyone would expect at a meal was that the senior guest by all accounts, Jesus, would wash the feet of anyone present, and the act has been understood as a gesture aimed at quieting their rivalry with one another.

Ancient spiritual leaders emphasized that the meal, with family and friends gathered together, was the perfect opportunity to bless God for His bounty. In the Gospels, Jesus' blessing over the meal is called "giving thanks" (Matt. 26:26, Mark 14:22, Luke 22:19, Luke 24:30). Paul, too, followed this custom (Acts 27:35), as do modern-day Jews.

The Polite Diner's Guide to Dipping and other Problems of Ancient Table Etiquette

Diners by the time of Jesus had use of knives and spoons (forks came into use only in the Middle Ages). But as is the custom in traditional societies, ancient diners served themselves by dipping into a common bowl or dish (Mark 14:20). Dipping was carried out with a modest-sized piece of bread or a palm leaf, but never with the finger. Several aspects of 'polite dipping' developed from this custom. "When there are two guests, they must wait for each other in taking food from the bowl. If there are three, he need not wait..." notes one source. Furthermore, "when two sit at a table, the senior guest should reach first for the food, and then the junior. If the junior reaches first, he is a glutton."

Dishes discovered in excavations at Jerash, Jordan

The rabbis did not mind criticizing those guilty of infractions of manners in the most graphic terms. The famed second century Rabbi Akiva took umbrage when an ill-mannered disciple held the stalk of a raw vegetable in his hand and bit into it with his teeth (instead of the proper way, which would have been to pluck off a piece with his hand) and admonished him sarcastically: "Don't do that, my son - go ahead and put your foot on the vegetable in the dish!" Akiva later confessed to his disciples that he had arranged the meal as test of the refinement of their general behavior.

A drinking cup was often shared at the meal though, hundreds of years before the discovery of germs, the rabbis already knew from experience that "a man should not drink from a cup and then pass it to his fellow, because it may endanger his fellow's life". At the very least, said one prominent sage, "wipe the [rim] before drinking, and wipe it again before putting it down."

Dishes

Pottery is one of the most valuable tools of the archaeologists in estimating the age of the communities they are excavating, as a change in culture usually heralded a change in the type of pottery used. Like today, people also used different kinds of dishes for different purposes. Most domestic pottery discovered consists of various sizes of bowls, making it likely that these were the vessels most often used for both eating and drinking. Amos in particular mentions drinking wine "by the bowlful" (Amos 6:6). Chalices also appeared on the scene from the 12th century BCE. Various kinds of decanters were used to serve wine. Those with a narrow neck, giving greater precision in pouring, indicate that the liquid within was of a particularly high value. Dippers, jugs used to dip from a large storage jar to a small one, have also been discovered in excavations.

A spoon discovered in the excavations at Masada.

Pottery first began to be used in around 6000 BCE. It was probably discovered by accident, when a fire on a clay floor turned the material into a hard material. The earliest potters made their vessels by hand, painting or incising them with varying patterns, including herringbone, zigzag, and triangles. From marks on the bottom of large jars dating from the Chalcolithic period (4300-3300 BCE) archaeologists can tell that they were turned on a straw mat. Coils of clay that looked like ropes adorned some of these pots, and may have also served to strengthen them. Sometimes the ancient potter even left fingerprints in the clay!

What did ancient people consider their "good dishes?" The Mishna gives us the answer in noting that the Sadducees, members of the wealthy upper class, "ate from dishes of silver and gold all their lives." Most people could afford some kind of glass dishes but only the rich could afford to purchase 'white glass', that is, glass free of all its impurities. In what was obviously an ancient form of welfare eligibility, community leaders in the early centuries after the time of Jesus devised a means of proving one had lowered one's standard of living and could apply for charity from the public purse: if he ate from gold dishes, then he would have to sell them and use the less expensive silver dishes; if he ate with bronze dishes, he would have to sell them for glass dishes. (The already poor man, however, was not

Bowls discovered at Qumran

Large storage vessels and a table from the Roman period discovered in excavations in the Burnt House in Jerusalem's Jewish Quarter.

required to sell his glass dishes for the most common dishes of all, those made out of clay.)

There was one more material out of which dishes were manufactured: stone. Stone jars and cups have been unearthed by archaeologists in the Jewish homes of Jerusalem's Herodian Quarter. Compared to clay dishes, stoneware was difficult and expensive to produce, and not particularly attractive. Their owners must therefore have had another reason to prefer them. John 2:6, among other ancient sources, gives us the reason: people believed that ritual impurity did not impart itself to stone implements.

Simply styled dishes and pots from the Roman era discovered in excavations at Jerash, Jordan

Kitchens as we know them today - rooms that combine the functions of eating, cooking, and storing food - did not exist in early Bible days. By Second Temple times in the Land of Israel, in wealthy homes there was a special room that was set aside for cooking, which contained an oven made of stone. The wealthy also had cooks in their employ. With regard to food storage, some houses had pantries where jars of grain, wine, and oil were stored, as well as utensils such as grinding stones of various sizes. Archaeologists have also found evidence of food storage, in the form of various kinds of storage jars and food remains, in locations throughout the ruins of houses they have excavated. And where was the dining room? Wealthier homes did indeed have dining rooms. But in smaller and simpler dwellings, people dined around a low table or a mat spread out in a multi-purpose room in what was often a one-room house. In fine weather, people ate in their courtyard or even on their rooftop.

Food was cooked in ovens constructed of clay, or a mixture of clay and straw, of various shapes and sizes. Some, shaped like upside-down cauldrons, were only used to bake bread, and other, larger versions, had a shelf above the cooking fire on which the pots of food could be placed. The ovens in simple homes were often located in courtyards, where the smoke and cooking smells could dissipate in the open air. Some houses did have ovens in enclosed rooms, which would have been used on winter days when the weather conditions were too severe to allow cooking outdoors. Foodstuffs, and utensils like pots and pans, serving spoons and ladles, were also stored in this room.

A display of kitchen utensils and a reconstructed ancient oven at Katzrin Mishnaic Village on the Golan Heights.

Dates

Pomegranates

The Seven Spe

"For the Lord your God is brin
with streams and pools of water
and hills; a land with wheat
pomegranates,
(Deutero

Wheat

B

Olives

Figs

of the Holy Land

ou into a good land – a land
springs flowing in the valleys
barley, vines and fig trees,
oil and honey.
8.7–8)

Grapes

Grain and Bread

"Give us by Day our Daily Bread" (Luke 11:3)

"As the rain and the snow come down from heaven and do not return to it without watering the earth and making it bud and flourish, so that it yields seed for the sower and bread for the eater, so is my word that goes out from my mouth" (Is. 55:10-11)

The Bible reports that Isaac reaped a harvest that was one hundred times what he had sown (Gen 26:12). By the time of this marvelous ingathering, somewhere at the beginning of the second millennium BCE, grain had already been cultivated in the Near East for thousands of years. In fact, the cultivation of grain began in this part of the world: hundreds of carbonized kernels of wheat and barley were discovered at a prehistoric site near the shores of the Sea of Galilee; carbonized kernels of wheat and barley were found by archaeologists also in one of the most ancient levels of the city of Jericho, dating back many millennia. Since grain does not grow wild in the Jericho oasis, we can assume the first farmers brought it from the mountains of Judea or Samaria and planted it there.

It is no coincidence that wheat and barley are first on the list of the Seven Species of Deuteronomy 8:8 - species for which the Land of Israel is known; much of the wheat grown throughout the world to this very day comes from a type of wheat genetically almost identical to a species that originated in the Holy Land. The species is known to botanists as emmer wheat, or more dramatically, "the mother of wheat." This was the name

given it by pioneering Jewish agronomist Aharon Aharonson, who rediscovered it growing in the mountains of Upper Galilee in the early twentieth century. Because the harvesting of wild wheat over the millennia had eventually mutated and changed the species significantly, Aharonson's find revolutionized wheat production throughout the world, as it enabled the genetic enrichment of modern wheat with a species close to the original strain.

Separating the wheat from the chaff

Barley, too, may have its origins in the Land of Israel, in a 'mother of barley' species known as Mount Tabor barley. In Bible days, barley, also used for fodder (1 Kings 4:28), was half the price of wheat, as indicated by its cost during the siege on Samaria by Ben Hadad King of Aram (2 Kings 7:1). The following saying in the Talmudic tractate *Shabbat* also indicates that barley was "good enough" but not as good as wheat: "he who can eat barley bread but eats wheat, violates 'do not destroy'" (Deut 20:19) - i.e., is guilty of waste. Barley was the last nourishment that could be obtained in a famine or in times of economic distress, as another Talmudic saying hints: "When the barley is quite gone from the jar, strife comes knocking at the door."

There is a scientific basis for the preference for wheat over barley: Compared to wheat, barley contains little

Harvesting grain.

gluten, the protein basis of the grain that allows the flour to rise. Barley bread, therefore, did not rise nicely, was coarse and hard of texture, and harder to chew and digest.

The Staff of Life

Grain has long been humanity's basic form of nourishment. The ripe golden kernels, which we know contain carbohydrates, proteins, fats, minerals, and vitamins, can be considered the perfect vegetable food source.

Significantly, the word for bread in Egyptian Arabic is *a'ash*, coming from the root word for life. This may possibly stem from a tradition regarding the Egyptian deity Osiris, one of whose names was "bread of humanity." Many deities in the ancient Near East were associated with grain, among them the Hittite god of the storm and the moon, and the Canaanite-Philistine Dagon (Judges 16:23, I Sam 5:2 *inter alia*). *Dagan,* the ancient Canaanite word for grain, came into the Hebrew language with its meaning unchanged. Recent excavations at Bethsaida, north of the Sea of Galilee, turned up an unexpected and fascinating find: a storm-

Separating the wheat from the chaff as it was done in Bible days.

moon god stele was unearthed in the gateway of the city dating from the 9th - 8th century BCE. Excavators have suggested that the area in front of which the stele was found may have been used as a threshing floor where religious rituals were also performed, of the type mentioned in 1 Kings 22: 10 and Hosea 9:1.

A grinder like this produced the flour for each day's supply of bread in Jesus' day.

But the ancients discovered that with all its advantages, grain could not easily be digested in its raw form. It was this realization that led them to discover the greatest advantage of this foodstuff - its versatility. Boil it in water, and it becomes gruel; bake it, and it becomes bread. And there are surprises: If it gets wet, don't throw it out! We will never know the identity of the ancient farmer who discovered that fact. He would not have been able to name the chemical process - fermentation - whereby the stored carbohydrates convert into sugar. But what happened when he tried baking his moist sprouted grain, grinding it and adding water? With a little yeast and the right conditions he had produced beer, the manufacture of which (often by women) appears both in Egyptian clay models and Mesopotamian texts.

Grain can be eaten fresh for a short period of time, when it is green and soft. This is the time, in early spring, when Jesus and the disciples were seen going through the field of "corn" (i.e., grain) on the Sabbath, plucking it and eating it as they walked (Matt 12:1, Mark 2:23, Luke 6:1). At this point, the grain is known as *carmel*, translated into English as "new grain." Grain was also eaten "parched", which meant toasting the kernels of grain over a fire for a short period of time (Lev 2:14). This favorite recipe of macrobiotic cooks of our day - we now know that toasting not only softens the grain, but also converts its starch into sweet-tasting dextrin - also appears in Ruth 2:14. When Jesse sent David down to his older brothers in the Valley of Elah where they faced the Philistine army, bread as well as parched grain was included in the supplies (1 Sam 17:17). Much later, when King David went out to fight his rebellious son Absalom, parched grain was also on hand in his military field kitchen (2 Sam. 17:28). In return for the magnificent cedar wood that adorned the Temple, King Solomon traded "twenty thousand cors of wheat for his household..." (1 Kings 5:11), and according to 2 Chron. 2:10, "twenty thousand cors of wheat and twenty thousand cors of barley" for the hewers of wood (a single cor was 200 liters).

"Bringing in the sheaves"

The Omer: Counting Your Blessings

In Lev. 23:9-16 we find a special ceremony associated with Passover and known as the offering of the Omer. An Omer is a measure of grain equal to about 6 gallons. On the first day after the Passover holiday had begun (or the first Sabbath thereafter - there was quite an argument going over this issue in Jesus' day between the Pharisees and the Saducees), a counting would begin which would end fifty days later with another holiday: Pentecost, which means "fifty" in Greek. The ripened "new grain" (Num. 28:26; Lev. 23:10) was brought to the Tabernacle (and later to the Temple) on Pentecost to entreat God's blessing on the harvest (Lev. 23:15-16).

Eventually, Jews began to associate the Feast of Weeks with the giving of the Ten Commandments at Sinai. Both events are of course mentioned in the Bible, but the giving of the Ten Commandments on the Feast of Weeks is a rabbinical assumption. The connection is based on the opening verse of Exodus 19, the story of the giving of the Ten Commandments: "In the third month after the Children of Israel were gone forth out of the land of Egypt, that same day came they into the wilderness of Sinai." "That same day," it was concluded, meant the day the Ten Commandments were given to Moses. Since, according to the Jewish calendar, this day coincided with the celebration of the Feast of Weeks, Pentecost became the "Festival of the Giving of Torah."

Not only anticipation, but also a certain degree of tension is contained in the counting. In later times, mourning ritual also became associated with this period of "the counting of the Omer", although no one can say why. Noga HaReuveni of Neot Kedumim Biblical Landscape Reserve believes that it is because the weather in the Holy Land is very capricious in this period. With everything from the "latter rains" to hail storms to heat waves, these fifty days were "ripe" with potential for either disaster or success of the harvest. For this reason, a portion of the successful harvest was "returned" to God in the form of a sacrifice,

A traditional plow

in thanksgiving, at Passover barley harvest (Lev. 23:10) and at Pentecost, as Ex. 34:22 commands, "Celebrate the Feast of Weeks with the First Fruits of the wheat harvest." Jeremiah chastises the Israelites for not giving due praise to God for the grain harvest, "They do not say to themselves, 'Let us fear the Lord our God, who gives autumn and spring rains in season, who assures us of the regular weeks of harvest' (Jer. 5:24).

Since barley was ready for harvest at Passover and wheat at Pentecost, we may understand that at the time of the barley harvest, the wheat was at a critical stage of its development, while at the time of the Pentecost wheat harvest, the summer fruits were at a critical stage of their own development. A saying at the time of Jesus, mandating strict observance of the biblical laws of bringing offerings of thanks to God went, "Bring the Omer (the new grain) at Passover so that the wheat will be blessed, and bring the offering of wheat at Pentecost so that the summer fruits will be blessed."

Sheaves of wheat

Barley and the Hebrew "Leap Year"

At the time of Jesus, the ripening of the barley had the power to determine the number of months in a particular year. The Jewish calendar is a lunar calendar, but in order to keep the holidays at the same time each year, and suit the lunar

Recreating the traditional baking of bread on a saj placed over the fire.

calendar to the agricultural year that went according to the sun, in some years an additional month would be added at the beginning of spring. In modern times, the month of Adar II is added at predetermined and known intervals. But in ancient times, the Sanhedrin would send emissaries into the barley fields to see if the barley was at a stage where it would be ripe for the harvest in time for Passover, the feast of the barley harvest. The ripened barley was known as "Abib" or "Aviv" (Ex. 13:4, 23:15, 34:18), today's modern Hebrew word for spring. If the barley had not reached the requisite maturity, the sages would decide, on this basis alone, to add another month.

The Best Gifts of the Earth and its Fullness (Deut 33:16)

According to Psalm 4:7, (and numerous other references) one of people's greatest joys is when "grain and new wine abound." Naturally, therefore, grain was one of the offerings acceptable on the altar in thanksgiving for a plentiful harvest.

The grain offering could be finely ground wheat (Lev. 2:1; 1 Chron. 21:23, Ezek 43:13) or barley (Ezek. 13). Toasted, crushed whole grain was the acceptable First Fruits offering (Lev. 2:12, Num. 15:21, Neh. 10:37). Olive oil, another of the Seven Species and another important fruit of the land, was often poured over the flour. Frankincense would add a pleasing aroma. Loaves (Lev. 23:17) or wafers (Exodus 29:23) could also be baked and given as offerings. These offerings were seasoned with salt, probably symbolic of the combination of bread and salt, the consumption of which sealed covenants in the ancient world. The grain or bread offering also helped support the priesthood, as the portion not consumed on the altar was given to the priests (Lev. 2:3,10; 7:9-10; Neh. 13.5). However this meal was no ordinary repast. To be eaten in a "holy place," it, too, had ritual significance.

Agricultural tools of a type used since Jesus' day.

Twelve large loaves of bread, each baked with four quarts of flour and known as the Bread of the Presence or the Showbread (Lev 24:5 *inter alia*) were placed on a table of gold "outside the veil" on the north side of the Tabernacle and in the Temple, in the Holy, or the outer room of the Holy of Holies.

A traditional farmer in the lowlands takes advantage of the breeze to help separate the wheat from the chaff.

The bread was a symbol of God's sustenance of the people, twelve loaves reminiscent of the Twelve Tribes of Israel. According to 1 Sam 21:6, David convinced Ahimelech the priest to allow him to partake of this bread, an incident recalled by Jesus when defending harvesting of grain on the Sabbath day (Matt. 12:3-4, Mark 2:25-26, Luke 6:3-4).

The family of priests known as the Kohathites were the bakers of the bread, bringing new loaves each Sabbath. In describing miracles associated with the Temple service, the Mishnah notes that when the old bread was removed to make way for the new, it was still as fresh as its first day on display.

From Stalk to Loaf

One of the ways of ensuring the blessings of the harvest was by fulfilling the injunction of Leviticus 23:22 to leave the edges of the field unharvested, so that the poor could help themselves to the gleanings. The sages were concerned that in their enthusiasm to obtain a bit of the ungleaned portions of the field, the gleaners would harm each other with the tools of the harvest, and therefore they determined that gleaning would be done by hand only.

The harvest was an event of paramount importance - a climax of the agricultural year and familiar to everyone who lived in the hill country of Judea, Samaria, and Galilee, and even in the sweltering valley of Jericho, where the harvest came earlier than in the rest of the country. For this reason, the harvest lent itself

Iron cutting and digging tools that were once fitted to wooden handles.

to symbolic meaning, which we can see in many New Testament verses (John 4:35, Rom 1:13, I Cor 9:10-12, Heb. 12:11 *inter alia*) and as a parable (Mark 12:2).

The Daily Grind

After the harvest and the threshing and winnowing of the grain, the grain would be stored, awaiting the grinding of an amount sufficient for each day's expected consumption. In most homes, grain was ground into flour by using a hand mill to produce flour. This first "food processor," a lowly grinding stone, was a tool so essential in the ancient household that it was forbidden to take it as a pledge against the return of a loan (Deut. 24:6).

A traditional rake used to separate the kernels of wheat or barley from their stalks.

After grinding, the flour was mixed with water and kneaded. It was then time to add the leavening (Matt. 13:33, Luke 13:21). Contrary to popular belief, leavening was not in the form in which we know it today. Leaven consisted of a piece of raw dough up to three weeks old, in which yeast had naturally developed. "Waiting for the bread to rise" was no short-term business. The Jerusalem Talmud reports that "the daughters of Lod would knead their bread, ascend to Jerusalem to pray, and return" in the space of the time it took for the bread to rise. This is important for us to realize when considering why the Children of Israel "did not have time" (Ex. 12:39) for their bread to rise before leaving Egypt, and so left it unleavened.

The preparation of bread was one of the hardest and most time-consuming of household activities. In order to have the bread baked and ready to take to the field, the housewife (Prov. 31:15) would have to rise long before dawn. In one hour of grinding, a mere 800 grams of flour can be produced. Assuming the consumption of about half a kilo

Wheel for grinding wheat/corn

Baking bread

of flour per person per day, it would take a housewife three hours to produce enough flour to feed a household of 5-6 people! If a bride has brought one female slave to her new husband's house, says the Mishnaic tractate *Ketubot*, she is free of the obligation to grind grain (along with baking and laundering).

The actual baking of the bread took only a few minutes. The simplest of ovens was a bed of coals (I Kings 19:6; Isa. 44:19), which eventually progressed into various types of freestanding convex structures made of clay or mud and

Baking bread in the ancient style in Cyprus

straw. Ovens were mainly located in the courtyards of houses, although larger ovens, operated by professional bakers, were known in the Roman period. The Talmud calls bread baked in a larger commercial oven *pat* (loaf) *pourni*, from the Latin word for oven, *furnus*. The most commonly available fuel in the Middle East was often animal dung, as mentioned in Ezekiel 4:15. However, when Jesus prepared a meal of bread and fish for the disciples on the shores of the Sea of Galilee after the Resurrection, a coal fire was used (John 21:9).

An old-style digging tool still used today by traditional farmers.

The fact that bread production was women's work (as well as all the ancient activities associated with bread production) is hidden in this gem from Tractate *Beresheet* of the Jerusalem Talmud, the words of a sage, Ben Zoma: "How hard the first man, Adam, must have labored before he could eat a bit of bread! He had to plow and sow and seed and hoe and reap and thresh, winnow and sift, grind, sift again, knead, moisten, and bake, and only after all this eat his bread. Whereas I get up in the morning and find my bread ready for me."

An understanding of the hard physical labor associated with bread production gives us a greater appreciation of the famous words "give us this day our daily bread" (Matt. 6:11). This was clearly not only a prayer for a good harvest or the means of purchasing the flour, but also an appeal for the stamina necessary to produce the bread.

Wheat
Triticum durum

"For the Lord your God is bringing you into a good land - a land with streams and pools of water, with springs flowing in the valleys and hills, a land with **wheat** and barley, vines and fig trees, pomegranates, olive oil and honey" (Deut. 8:7-8)

Barley
Hordeum vulgare

"So Naomi returned from Moab accompanied by Ruth the Moabitess, her daughter-in-law, arriving in Bethlehem as the **barley** harvest was beginning" (Ruth 1:22)

After the destruction of the Temple, unique religious obligations devolved on Jewish women during the baking of bread. The Talmudic tractate *Taanit* describes the housewife's duty to bake two loaves of bread before the Sabbath, the double portion symbolic of the double portion of manna the Israelites received in the desert on the Sabbath, or because of the Showbread displayed each Sabbath in the Tabernacle and the Temple (Lev 24:8-9; I Sam 21:7). After the destruction of the Temple, before baking the bread, the housewife removed a bit of the dough and threw it separately into the fire, as a reminder of the sacrifices that were once made in the Temple.

Let Them Eat "Cake"

Several kinds of bread are mentioned in the Bible. The "loaf" of Exodus 29:23 - whose Hebrew name *kikar* indicates that it had a round shape, was probably quite similar in appearance to pita bread as we know it today. This was likely to have been the form of the "loaves" of Mark 6:38 as well. This simple bread, round and slightly irregular in shape, resembled the flat, light colored stones that are strewn across the limestone hills of the Holy Land. It is therefore no coincidence that we find an association between stones and bread in the Gospels: "Which of you, if his sons ask for bread, will give him a stone?" (Matt. 7:9). And when Jesus was fasting in the wilderness for 40 days, the devil couched his temptation in this case in terms of the rocky surroundings: "The tempter came to him and said, 'if you are the Son of God, turn these stones into bread'" (Matt 4:3).

Cake, another kind of biblical bread, did not have the sweet connotation the word has today, but its Hebrew name comes from another word for "round." It seems to have been baked directly on the fire. The "wafer" (Ex. 29:23, Lev. 8:26, Num. 6:19) was similar to the cake, but thinner. Bread could come in various shapes, and ancient "designer" bread molds show that bread could also be an elegant element in a meal. A fish-shaped bread mold, with the relief design of fish scales in the bottom, was discovered in the kitchen

A child sits atop a sledge to add the weight to help separate the kernels from their stalks in this traditional village. Deut. 25:4 states that an animal was not to be muzzled during this work, to allow it to feed. Behind the child is a large grinder.

of a palace in Mari (ancient Assyria) dating from around 1800 BCE.

Symbolism: When Bread becomes... "Bread"

A girl in period costume tries her hand at grinding grain in the ancient manner.

Bread was the "stay" and "staff" of human existence, as noted poetically in some translations of Isaiah 3:1 and Ezekiel 4:16. It was the food of kings (2 Kings 25:29), farmers' fare in the field (Ruth 2:14) and to be eaten while on a journey or away from home (Mark 6:8). Bread is mentioned repeatedly throughout the Bible, starting with Genesis 3:19 where the word is mistranslated - or transformed directly into its symbolic state - as "food." Bread was an important element in the ceremonies of the Tabernacle (Numbers 28:2) and later the Temple (1 Samuel 21:6). As a biblical metaphor - "the bread of wickedness" (Prov. 4:17) means all wicked things. The proverbial "woman of valor" is busy all day, therefore she does not eat "the bread of idleness" (Prov. 31:27).

What became a metaphor for many of us who are divorced from the soil was far from a literary allusion to the ancients: When famine struck, ancient farmers were faced with an agonizing decision. What to do with the last seeds of grain? If they ground them into flour to bake bread, there would be no seeds to sow for next year's crop. If they set them aside to sow, they would be depriving their loved ones of a nourishing meal. As some farmers sowed their last seeds, perhaps Psalm 126:5 expressed their hope for a better future, "they that sow in tears shall reap in joy."

The Blessing over the Bread

Jesus is recorded in the Gospels "giving thanks" for the bread, notably at the Last Supper, (Matt 26:26, Mark 14:22, Luke 22:19) and on the road to Emmaus (Luke 24:30). The giving of thanks, hinted at by Psalm 104:14 and first set down in writing in the early years after the time of Jesus, is almost identical to the prayer said today in Jewish homes, where bread is still traditionally "broken" and given to everyone at the table. "Blessed are you O Lord our God, King of the Universe, who brings forth bread from the earth." Commentators have noted that the traditional blessing says "brings forth bread" and not "brings forth wheat" because of the on-going partnership between human beings and God.

Children grinding and sifting grain. In ancient times, these tasks were the work of the women of the household.

Hosea also uses leavening as a symbol: He describes wicked people as "...an oven heated by a baker. He ceases stirring the fire after kneading the dough, until it is leavened" (Hos. 7:4). Medieval Jewish commentator Rashi explains this verse: "Whoever thinks in his heart to do evil he rests on [his plans] until morning, like a baker stops his kneading of the dough until it rises and he can bake it." Paul, who refers in 1 Corinthians 5:8 to "the leaven of malice and wickedness", could certainly have agreed with this interpretation.

Bread normally baked at home, in a courtyard oven in full view of everyone in the house hold, became a powerful symbol because of its very commonality.

Traditionally baked pita bread.

Like wine, at the Last Supper Jesus transformed bread into an enduring part of Christian theology and practice. And the discourse on bread in John 6:30-58 includes the famous words "I am the bread of life; he that cometh to me shall never hunger...." It was the commonality of bread in everyday life that allowed it to become the potent symbol that it did.

Jesus also found leavening useful as a symbol because it actively changes that of which it becomes a part. Matthew 16:5-12 records that Jesus warns the disciples against false teachings, called by Jesus "the leaven of the Pharisees and the Saducees".

EZEKIEL'S MULTI-GRAIN BREAD

"Take wheat and barley, beans and lentils, millet and spelt; put them in a storage jar and use them to make bread for yourself." (Ezek 4:9)

God commanded Ezekiel to bake this bread, as part of God's message of doom to the people of Jerusalem. Spelt is a kind of wheat not available in most places in the west, so it has not been included in the ingredients below. Broad bean flour and lentil flour can be purchased in health food stores or stores specializing in products for the Indian cuisine. Remember that leavening in Bible days was not yeast as we know it today! To be truly biblical, use 1 tsp. leftover dough from your last batch of Ezekiel's bread, or, instead of water, use freshly pressed grape juice or freshly made applesauce; both fruits have natural yeast on their skins.

1/2 cup barley flour
1/4 cup finely ground broad bean flour
1/4 cup millet flour
1 cup durum wheat flour
1/2 cup finely ground lentil flour
1 tsp salt
1/4 cup olive oil
1 tsp. biblical leavening or fruit juice (with peel)
water

Mix all the ingredients together. Add the olive oil, leavening, and water as needed to form the dough. Knead and allow to rise for two hours in a warm place. Knead again.
Form into flat round loaves the size of pita bread and bake on coals until golden brown, turning once, for about 10 minutes.

A grinder

The Fruit of the Vine

"A choice vine of sound and reliable stock" (Jer. 2:21)

"As when juice is still found in a cluster of grapes and men say, 'Don't destroy it, there is yet some good in it'" (Is. 65:8)

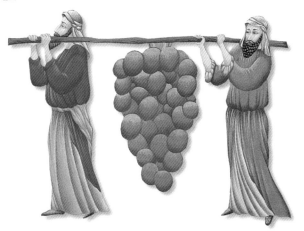

The spies sent by Moses present the excellent (and heavy) fruit of the Land of Israel (Num. 13:23). Drawing by Oleg Trabish

Unlike grain, grapes are not a commodity necessary for human survival. Yet the fruit of the vine, which both "makes life merry" (Eccl. 10:19) and "gladdens the heart" (Ps. 104:15) is the origin of numerous memorable biblical images, attaining stature as much for its social and cultural aspects as for its nutritional value.

Botanists place the origin of the Mediterranean grapevine growing in the Holy Land, *vitis vinifera sylvestris*, somewhere in the hills of Armenia between the Caspian and the Black Sea. Evidence of its cultivation in various locations in the Ancient Near East extends back at least to the third millennium BCE, and when Egypt ruled Canaan in the Late Bronze age, the centuries before the Israelites came into the Land, the Egyptians imported fine-quality wine from Canaan. Genesis 9:20 accurately reflects the antiquity of viniculture: grapes were the first plant placed in the ground by Noah after the flood. (As Genesis 9:20 relates, Noah was also the first man in biblical history to suffer the consequences of drinking too much.)

The Land of Israel enjoys all the advantages of the vine-friendly climate zone shared by other wine-producing countries like Greece, Italy, France, and California. While the grapes are still unready to harvest, when they are small and acidic they are called *boser* - the "sour grapes" of Isaiah 18:15, Ezekiel 18:2, and Jeremiah 31:29-30.

Genesis 49:11 says of Judah, "He will tether his donkey to a vine, his colt to the choicest branch; he will wash his garments in wine, his robes in the blood of grapes." We

may understand from these references that the territory of the Tribe of Judah was prime grape-growing country - that the vines will be so strong that a beast of burden could be tied to them, and wine will be so plentiful that there will be no need of water to wash clothing! Ancient terraces still cover the hillsides for miles all around the central Judean town of Ein Karem, the traditional birthplace of John the Baptist, whose name means "the spring of the vineyard."

The Bible tells us that the time of the grape harvest, was a joyous time. Judges 9:27 reports of the men of Shechem, "After they had gone out into the fields and gathered the grapes and trodden them, they held a festival in the temple of their god." Isaiah 16:10 describes the desolation of Moab in these terms: "Joy and gladness are taken away from the orchards; no one sings or shouts in the vineyards; no one treads out wine at the presses." The famous story of the capture of the virgins at Shiloh by the outcast Benjaminites took place during the feast undoubtedly connected with the grape harvest (Judges 21:91-21).

Like all other agricultural elements, the great joy of the successful harvest was translated into thanksgiving to God for making it possible. In fact, an abundance of wine, among other products, was the proof that the Children of Israel had fulfilled the will of God (Deut. 7:12). Wine was

Harvest time in the vineyard.

therefore one of the offerings to be brought daily to the altar (Ex. 29:38), as well as on holidays (Lev. 23:13) and in fulfillment of special vows (Num. 15:10).

From Vine to Wine

Archaeologists working in the Holy Land have uncovered hundreds of open-air grape presses throughout the hill country. The advantage of working outdoors was the ability to make use of daylight, to avoid construction of a building, and to allow fermentation fumes to quickly dissipate in the fresh air. The very first grape press was none other than the human foot, the gentle touch of which avoided the breakage of the pip (the inner part containing the oil, seeds, and tannins). In the Roman era, screw presses began to appear, but pressing by foot was still the norm, and Joseph's dream describes how he hand-pressed grapes into Pharaoh's cup (Gen. 40:11). Like so many other aspects of grape production - and food in the Bible in general - the press, too, became a symbol: "I have trodden the winepress alone," says Isaiah 63:3, "from the nations no-one was with me: I trampled them in my anger and trod them down in my wrath; their blood spattered my garments, and I stained all my clothing." In Roman times, wine began to be imported to the Holy Land from Cyprus (even the incense for use in the Temple service was manufactured using Cyprus wine) and from Rhodes. Wine originating from grapes grown in the Sharon Plain was known to be weak, while wine from Carmel grapes, from Ammon in Transjordan, and from Italy, was considered stronger. In recent excavations at Bethsaida near the Sea of Galilee, a house with a wine cellar was discovered, presumably belonging to a Roman-era wine-maker. But this vintner's own next-door neighbor was for some mysterious reason not a customer - wine amphorae from Rhodes were discovered in his house!

Wine-Making

Wine production is basically a simple process requiring two elements, grapes and yeast. The yeast occurs naturally in the skin of the grape and when the skin of the grape is broken when the grapes are trodden, the yeast begins to act, converting

Treading grapes in a winepress at the time of Jesus

Hundreds of ancient winepresses like this one have been discovered throughout the hill country of Israel.

the sugar of the grape juice into alcohol. During the fermentation process, carbon dioxide is formed. It drives oxygen, detrimental to the wine, to the surface, which causes the wine to boil and bubble. A major concern of the ancient winemaker was to allow the carbon dioxide to escape without prolonged contact with the air which risks contamination from a fungus that converts the alcohol into vinegar. Roman-era naturalist and historian Pliny the Elder reported that resin from the terebinth tree was added to the wine to prevent this particular disaster. The ancient vintner had to leave his grape juice exposed to air long enough to let the carbon dioxide out without letting too much air in. This might well have made the difference between "good wine" and "that which is worse" (John 2:10).

Red or White? And Many More Hues

The fact that most of the wine that our biblical forefathers drank was red may be deduced from the many biblical passages connecting blood with grapes, among them Deut. 32:14, Ezek. 19:10, Isaiah 49:26. The power in this symbol is perhaps best known from Jesus when he raised the goblet of wine at the Last Supper with the words "this is my blood" (Matt 26:27-28, *et al*). Another hint of the color of the most common wine is one of the Hebrew words for the fruit of the vine - hamra, which comes from a Hebrew word for a hue of red. Scientists now understand that a recessive gene produces white grapes. These were rare in the early generations of wine making and did not become common until trade routes expanded, allowing vintners to obtain new strains of grapes from distant locations. White wine does not appear in written sources until the period of the Ptolemies. But the ancient Egyptians were familiar with a wide palate of wine colors, including not only red, but also pink, green, deep red, and deep blue, depending on the type of grapes used.

Vinegar was manufactured from what was known as "flat wine," probably produced by pouring water over mashed grapes. Dried figs, salt, and honey could be added to this mixture. It was much more diluted than wine, making it a good commodity for a journey, where, as a beverage, a little would go a long way (although, as one could imagine, it was not particularly tasty, as can be deduced from Proverbs 10:26 and Psalm 69:21).

Details of the mosaic of the Church of Saints Lot and Procopius near Mount Nebo, showing the grape harvest and pressing.

The Talmud notes the existence of some 60 different kinds of wine, and the first century CE naturalist Pliny extends this list to 80, while Strabo has a list of 130! The Bible also differentiates between types of wine, including Hosea's "wine from Lebanon" (Hos. 14:8), apparently known for its fine bouquet, "wine from Helbon" (Ezek. 27:18) imported from Damascus. Archaeologists discovered a collection of pottery shards in Samaria from the eighth century BCE, the period of the Israelite kingdom, in which 20 of the 63 letters mention shipments of wine. An inscription on a clay jar discovered at Hazor in the Galilee, also from the period of the Israelite kingdom, was marked as *smadar* wine - young wine - belonging to Pekah son of Remaliah (2 Kings 15:27 *inter alia*). In David's administration, one official was in charge of the vineyards and winestores of the king (I Chron. 27:27).

The harvest of these ripening clusters is only days away.

Good for What Ails You - Up to a Point

Wine enjoyed wide use as a component in medical treatment. For example, wine was part of the poultice applied by the Good Samaritan to the injured man, as reported in Luke 10:34: " So he went to him and bandaged his wounds, pouring on oil and wine..." That wine could be beneficial was also known to the Apostle Paul who recommended to Timothy: "...use a little wine for your stomach's sake and your frequent infirmities" (1 Tim. 5:23).

Hippocrates, the fifth century Greek father of modern medicine, was very interested in the effects of wine on the human body. He noted that red wine and boiled wine had good effects on digestion, while white wine was beneficial to the bladder. However he warned his patients to stay away from sweet wine, which he believed led to swelling of the stomach. Pliny, the Roman naturalist, recommended applying wine to scorpion, spider, and bee stings. The Roman doctor Gallus, whose thriving practice revolved around treating unfortunate gladiators wounded in the ring, noted that applications of wine prevented gangrene.

In spite of wine's beneficial medicinal effects, Jewish sages of the late Roman period repeatedly point their finger at intoxication as the root of all sins. So did Ephesians 5:18 which instructs "Do not get drunk on wine, which leads to debauchery", and 1 Peter 4:3 which speaks of drunkenness as an excess of the pagans. Some even suggested that "the tree whose fruit Adam ate was a vine, for nothing brings as much woe to a man as wine."

Detail of a mosaic from Cyprus depicting ripe grapes on the vine.

33

Vines growing in the Jordan Valley.

Later Jewish sages also noted the benefits of wine in small quantities, and that it was harmful in large amounts. In a commentary on the book of Leviticus, one sage, Rabbi Tanhuma said: "Wine - its own mother (i.e. the vine) cannot stand up under the weight of the juice in the grapes, and you expect to stand up under it? Though the vine is propped up with many reeds and many pronged rods, it cannot stand up and sags under the weight of the juice of the grapes. And you expect to stand up under wine?" And one of the earliest descriptions of a hangover anywhere may be found in the Talmudic tractate *Nedarim*, where one of the sages describes it as "a tight cord around my head from Passover to Pentecost".

Wine as a Symbol

Two memorable biblical passages, Isaiah 5 and Ezekiel 17:5-8, demonstrate the hard work of viniculture by turning it into a metaphor to which every grape-grower and probably every farmer of every ilk could relate, then and now. Isaiah 5, the "Song of the Vineyard", is a veritable farmer's almanac of grape-growing, with every element, from the terracing to the planting to the guarding to the grapes that were "bad," and more, placed in the service of the prophet as a symbol of God's care for His people, and the disappointing results.

No matter how skilled the farmer, the first few clusters of grapes would not appear for five years, and a marketable product not for an entire decade! It is an amazing thought to the modern mind that the ancient farmer (who only lived about forty years) might spend up to one-sixth of his life cultivating his vineyards. This was work for settled people, not nomads. Jeremiah highlights this fact in describing the ascetic, tent-dwelling Rechabites as people who neither drink wine "...nor sow seed, nor plant vineyard,...but ...dwell in tents..."(Jer 35:7)

Precisely because it took so long to grow, the vine and its cultivation was a biblical symbol of peace: "each man under his vine and his fig tree" (1 Kings 4:25) is the Bible's way of describing the peaceful days of the reign of Solomon.

Beating "spears into pruning hooks" (Isa. 2:4, Micah 4:3) is one of the best-known scriptural references to an end to warfare. During the siege on Jerusalem by the Assyrians Rabshakeh, the Assyrian commander, tempts its citizens to surrender by offering them what was obviously the ultimate peacetime reward, " land of bread and vineyards" (2 Kings 18:32).

On the other hand, eating the first small grapes that appear each season - small and acidic and therefore extremely unpleasant to the taste - became a symbol of committing sin: the "sour grapes" of Isaiah 18:2, Jeremiah 31:29-30 and Ezekiel 18:2.

Adding water to pressed grape skins and pressing again yielded a poor type of wine that was supplied to workers and known as *tamad* - perhaps vinegar - but this was a drink to be avoided (Isa 1:22). Wine unmixed with water was obviously the strongest form of the drink and became a metaphor in Revelations 14:10: "He too will drink the wine of God's fury, which has been poured full strength into the cup of his wrath..."

And why does "no one put new wine into old wine skins?" (Mark 2:22) Chemistry is behind that famous metaphor. Wine might be moved into wineskins for transport before all the carbon dioxide, formed during the fermentation process had escaped. If that was the case, old skins, which had lost their flexibility, would burst at the seams and the precious liquid would be lost. New skins, however, could stretch, accommodating the carbon dioxide fumes. This idea is reflected in Job 32:19-20: when his friend Elihu can't keep quiet any longer he expresses his frustration by saying, "Inside I am like bottled-up wine, like new wineskins ready to burst."

Flavoring Wine

What Amos 9:13, and Joel 1:5 called "new wine", *assis* in Hebrew, was a drink created during the process of fermentation; once the alcohol reaches 14% the fermentation

Detail of a mosaic from Cyprus depicting a wine vessel.

Dates also produced a tasty wine in ancient times.

stops, the last remaining yeast dies off. Then, sweetened wine could be made by adding raisins, honey, or some other fruit juice as a sweetening agent. This may be "the nectar of my pomegranate" mentioned in Song of Songs 8:2, Isaiah 65:11 and Proverbs 23:30. Among the various spices added to wine by the ancients, one source, Columella, suggests adding crushed iris to the wine and another recipe suggests cardamom and saffron. The Song of Songs 8:2 also mentions wine flavored with various spices. According to Mark 15:23, wine mixed with myrrh was offered to Jesus on the Cross.

Other Beverages in Bible Times

Beer may be one of the oldest intoxicating beverages known to humanity. Some scholars believe its production may have begun in Mesopotamia and Egypt, as far back as the first domestication of grain, its essential ingredient. An early recipe for beer appears in the writings of a fourth century BCE chemist in Alexandria, Egypt. It is exactly the same way that to this day beer known as Bouze is manufactured in Sudan (which, by the way gives us the English word booze). Beer is much more characteristic of Mesopotamia and Egypt where grapes did not grow well. It never became popular in the Land of Israel; the Greeks considered it a barbarian beverage, and passed this prejudice on to the Romans.

According to Pliny, the ancient inhabitants of the Land of Israel in the days of Jesus might have enjoyed date wine. Dates have double the sugar of grapes; sufficient amounts of juice can be expressed when trodden, and the wild yeasts on the date skins can contribute to the fermenting of the beverage. Wine was also made from other fruits, such as

Rachel and Jacob at their first meeting at the well. Drawing: Oleg Trabish.

the extinct and mysterious balsam plant and the more familiar apples, figs and pomegranates. A whiff of slightly overripe end-of-summer carobs still hanging from today's trees in the Judean Mountains or Galilee reveals the yeasty odor that tells us that this fruit, too, could be turned into an alcoholic beverage.

The holes in the spout of this vessel are for straining out residue from a liquid, probably of beer.

Living Water

In the dry climate of the Holy Land as indeed today, perhaps no commodity was higher on the list of importance in Biblical life than water. In the days of the Patriarchs and the Matriarchs, Abraham and Isaac quarreled with the herdsmen of Gerar over the ownership of wells at Beersheba in the Negev, as related in Genesis 21:30 and 26:20-22. The well was the most important social gathering place in every village, town, or tribal territory, and therefore it is not surprising to find that Abraham's servant found Isaac's future wife at the well (Gen. 24:11) and that Jacob also found his beloved Rachel, when she came to draw water for her flock (Gen. 29:10).

Drawing water from a well

At the archaeological site of Tel Beersheva is a 210-meter deep well, the deepest ever discovered from its time, dug at least 3000 years ago. Water jars, many of them very large, have been discovered in excavations throughout Israel, as water had to be brought every day from the nearest spring and stored for convenient use in the courtyards of people's homes.

Water played a significant role during the wanderings of the Children of Israel in the Sinai Desert. At Rephidim, when the people were "thirsty for water" (Ex. 17:3) God told Moses to strike the rock to produce water. Later, at Kadesh, a similar event occurred, when God told Moses to speak to the rock, but Moses struck it. For disobeying God in this matter, Moses was forbidden to enter the Land of Israel (Numbers 20:8-12).

Drawing water from a well in Sinai.

The storage of water in cisterns and elaborate systems constructed to conduct it there from springs or surface runoff is a hallmark of a strong central government that could rally and pay the force needed to carry out the work. Such systems, born of the intense need for a constant supply of water and the genius of their engineers, have been discovered at such important biblical sites as Jerusalem, Gibeon, Gezer, Megiddo, Hazor, Beersheba, and many more.

One look at the depth of some of these water shafts, and the steep flights of stairs that led to them can help us understand what a strenuous task it must have been to bring the water from the bottom of the shaft to the city. It was hardly a desirable way to make a living, as we see from the story of the Gibeonites, a Canaanite people who lied to Joshua about their origins to save their lives. When he discovered their deception, he allowed them to live, but said to them, "you are now under a curse. You will never cease to work as woodcutters and water carriers for the house of my God" (Josh. 9:23).

Hezekiah's Tunnel in Jerusalem, hewn to protect the city's water from the attacking Assyrians (2 Chron. 32:3).

The Pool of Siloam at the exit of Hezekiah's Tunnel (Neh. 3:15, John 9:7)

Modern scientists have wondered about the detrimental effects of the bacteria that were sure to develop in water stored over a long period. (The Holy Land goes for a full eight months with no rain.) Some suggest that the storage of water in covered cisterns, which were dark, would preclude the development of bacteria that needed light to survive. The mixing of water with wine, common in Bible days, may have also had the effect of killing off bacteria in water stored over a long period.

Because of the supreme importance of water to life, it lent itself to symbolism like no other biblical symbol. Numerous references to water as a symbol of salvation, and of life itself, are scattered through the books of the Prophets and the New Testament. "With joy will you draw water from the wells of salvation," promised Isaiah in 12:3. Jeremiah equates God with "the spring of living water" (Jer. 2:13, 17:13), and Jesus also speaks of "living water" when talking to the Samaritan woman at the well of Shechem (John 4:10). Bathing with water was much more than a hygienic practice to biblical people; it symbolized inner purification (Lev. 15:13 *inter alia*). Such ritual immersion, with all its symbolism, made its way from Judaism into Christianity via the ministry of John the Baptist.

SPICED WINE

"I would give you spiced wine to drink, the nectar of my pomegranates." (Song of Songs 8:2)

1/2 cup white wine	1 stick cinnamon
6 ozs honey	2 dates
1 bay leaf	4 pints white wine

Heat 1/2 cup white wine with the honey until dissolved. Remove from heat. Add the bay leaf, cinnamon and chopped dates. Add the remaining wine and simmer for one hour, stirring occasionally.
Before serving remove bay leaf and cinnamon stick. Can be served hot or at room temperature.

Olives

"The Lord called you a thriving olive tree with fruit beautiful in form" (Jer. 11:16)

"They said to the olive tree, 'Be our king.' But the olive tree answered, 'Should I give up my oil, by which both gods and men are honored, to hold sway over the trees?'"
(Judges 9:8-9)

An olive tree, gnarled with age, in the Garden of Gethsemane in Jerusalem.

Today we consider olives and olive oil mainly foodstuffs. But in Bible days, olive oil had many additional uses that made it important and placed it on the prestigious list of the Seven Species of Deuteronomy 8:8. Olive oil was the indispensable fuel of the Land of the Bible. It was a pleasing offering to God in the Tabernacle (Ex. 29:40), a practice later continued in the Temple service. It was the anointing oil of kings (1 Sam. 10:1) and priests (Ex. 29:7), a cosmetic (Ecc. 9:8) and a medicine (Isa. 1:6; Mark 6:13; Luke 10:34). Considering the myriad benefits, it is no wonder that in Jotham's Fable in Judges 9:8 it is the first tree to which the others turn to be their king. Hosea speaks of its "splendor" (Hos. 14:6), and Jeremiah 11:16 calls it "thriving...with fruit beautiful in form."

A wild strain of olives, the *Olea europaea*, grows in the forests of the Land of Israel, and was almost certainly the first domesticated species of olive in the world. Olive pits have been found in excavations as early as the Chalcolithic period (4300-3300 BCE) and the Bronze Age (fourth and third millennium BCE) levels of the important biblical cities of Megiddo, Gezer, Lachish, and Beit Shean.

"Oil from the Flinty Rock" (Deut. 32:13)

The Galilee and Judean mountains, with their average annual rainfall of 400-500 millimeters and year-round cool nights, are perfect for the raising of olives. When the Israelites came into the land, it was promised they would find olive orchards (Deut. 6:11), and Deuteronomy 33:24 hints that that the territory of Asher was prime olive country at the time of the Bible, as it is today.

As the ancients grew wiser in the ways of agriculture, they realized that in their natural state the rocky hillsides were not spacious enough to raise quantities of fruits or vegetables. They therefore created "stepped fields" or terraces, many of which have remained in place to this day. In the Judean mountains, large-scale construction of terraces began in the late Iron Age (eighth-sixth centuries BCE). It was during this period that the Northern Kingdom of Israel was destroyed by the Assyrians, in 721 BCE, when an influx of refugees from the north swelled the population of the city. This was the driving force behind agricultural development in the surrounding countryside.

Olive trees blossom in May, and the fate of the flower was one of the constant concerns of the biblical farmer during the Omer, the fifty-day period between Passover and Pentecost, when searing winds blowing in from the desert could ruin them (Job 15:33). If all goes well, the harvest takes place around the end of October. Traditionally, olives were harvested by beating the branches with sticks (Deut. 24:20). By the time of Jesus, this practice had been gradually

The crushing stone and basin of an olive oil press.

The olive harvest, a family affair, takes place in the fall.

replaced, for the good of the tree and the fruit, by the more gentle method of shaking the branches. Any olives that did not fall off by the second rainfall of autumn using this method of harvesting were to be left for the poor. By that time, any olives left would have turned black. People are sometimes surprised to discover that the black olives they enjoy are nothing but very ripe green ones!

Since antiquity, farmers have grafted wild olives from the forest onto an existing rootstock of a particular tree that they could depend on to produce fine fruit. This method has given the New Testament one of its most enduring symbols: the "grafted-on" branches of Romans 11:17, symbolizing the bond, through the Christian faith, of Gentiles to God. Olive trees live to a very great age. Out of the old trunk, the farmer trains a "shoot" (Isa. 11:1). This Hebrew word, *netzer*, is the root of the Hebrew name of the city of Nazareth. The Hebrew word for Christian, *Notzri*, also comes from this word. The wood of the olive tree also found many uses. From its thinner branches, baskets were woven. The thicker portions of the wood have beautiful undulating patterns in varying shades of brown, and were therefore much in demand for furniture

For hundreds of years, the richly hued wood of the olive tree has provided the raw material from which Holy Land craftsmen produce statues of biblical figures.

Most of the oil seeps from the crushed olives when they are placed in a column of baskets, seen here, on which pressure is exerted for an extended period.

and in building. The entrance to the inner sanctuary of the First Temple had doors made of carved olive wood (I Kgs. 6:31-35).

The oil from the fruit was not the only aspect of the tree connected with light. The olive leaf shines in the sun with a beautiful silvery gleam. An ancient legend relates that when the angels told Sarah that she was to give birth after her long years of barrenness, "her face shone like an olive [leaf]." In the Old Testament, olive oil production is mentioned specifically only twice, in Joel 2:24 where a vat to collect the oil is mentioned, and in Micah 6:15, which refers to crushing of the fruit. Painful as it may sound when considering how hard an olive is, in Greek, there is a special word for the shoe to be worn when treading olives (a practice reflected in certain translations of Micah 6:15) and on the island of Corsica, the treading of olives by foot was observed until recent times. Scholars therefore believe that in the earliest stages of the history of oil production, olives were pressed by foot, much like grapes. But as the industry advanced, the crushing stone became the norm.

"Oil from Pressed Olives" (Nu. 28:6)

Oil production had three basic stages: Crushing the olives to a mash, pressing the mass to extract the fluid, and the rising of the lighter oil onto the surface of the watery lees, accomplished by pouring the liquid from vessel to vessel until it was separated. We know that the ancients wasted very little of their resources, and therefore even the lees had its uses, as fertilizer for the olive trees, and poured over grain to protect it from insects and mice, and even as a component in plaster, where second-century BCE statesman Cato (author of a treatise on agriculture) says it kept insects away and prevented the earth from becoming muddy.

The olive oil considered by connoisseurs today to be the best and most nutritious is produced by the cold-press method, although in large industrial oil-production plants today, olives are often heated to express them more readily from the fruit. This process, well-known in antiquity, was carried out in the grove-owner's home before the olives were taken to the press. The grove owners did not always own their own presses; sometimes a privately owned or cooperative press would serve a whole area. The olives went through three pressings: the first stage produced the purest oil, while a second and third pressing continued the process of expression, which was completed over a twenty-four hour period.

In the first stage of production, the olives were poured into the round crushing mill, and crushed by a round upper stone attached to a beam and pushed around by either human or animal power. From here, the crushed olives were scooped up, inserted into round baskets and placed one atop the other over a round basin, or press-bed, built into the floor, with pressure on this column of baskets exerted by a screw. This method, in use to the present day, came into vogue in the century before Jesus. Before this time, most of the oil was pressed by a wooden beam inserted into a recess in the wall, which hung over the basin. The "fulcrum" of the beam was the column of flat baskets. On the beam were hung weights of 600 pounds each that could be lowered into niches in the floor. The floor around the press-bed was inclined towards it, to allow excess oil to flow back into it.

When the olives had been squeezed of as much oil as possible, they still had not outlived their usefulness. The pits contained enough oil to be used as fuel, a common method of heating ovens during the Roman times. The olive oil press is called in Aramaic *Gat Shamna*. Transmitted via the Greek to the English, this gives us the Gethsemane of the New Testament (Matt. 26:36; Mark 14:32). Scholars have pointed out that Jesus and the Disciples sought out Gethsemane on the fateful night before Jesus' arrest as a place that would be deserted even in a Jerusalem crowded with pilgrims for the holiday because, during the Passover season, the olive press would have been inoperative and the area deserted. Interpreters of Scripture also see the crushing stone that was part of every olive press as taking on a new meaning in the context of Jesus' experience of sweating blood at Gethsemane.

The ancient Jewish sources mention many ways to eat olives. "Live" olives were apparently eaten after being nominally processed by pickling only in salt. These must have been the very ripest of the fruit that after being dried lose the bitter taste that makes other olives almost impossible to the palate.

An "old-fashioned" stone-hung press at Beit Guvrin, a method that went out of style by Jesus' day in favor of the screw-press.

"He makes a treaty with Assyria and sends olive oil to Egypt" (Hos. 12:1)

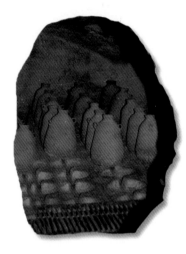

At the time of Jesus, olive oil was commonly stored in jars like these, found in a cave at Beit Guvrin in the Judean lowlands. The jars were placed in hollows connected by channels so that spilled oil could be salvaged.

In terms of trade, olive oil was one of the most significant exports of the Land of Israel. Early Bronze Age jugs and jars from Canaan have been discovered in Egypt and by the Late Bronze Age, a style of jar typical of olive oil storage was also found in Greece. The second-century Greek historian Xenon reports that olive trees flourished in the gardens of the pharaohs during the thirteenth century BCE. King Solomon traded olive oil for cedars from King Hiram of Tyre (I Kgs. 5:11), and perfumed olive oil was among the treasures which King Hezekiah showed the envoys of the king of Babylon (2 Kgs. 20:13; Isa. 39:2). Trade in olives, interrupted by the destruction of the First Temple, was resumed in the days of Zerubabel (Ezra 3:7).

In the New Testament, oil is one of the commodities sold in the market (Matt. 25:9), and was used as a means of payment (Luke 16:6; Rev. 18:13). Roman-era historian and naturalist Pliny has high praise for the olives of the land of Israel, stating that while they were smaller and less meaty than the olives of Egypt, they produced a great deal of oil, and were therefore exported to Italy.

The Olive as a Symbol

A good name, say correct translations of Ecclesiastes 7:1, is better than "fragrant oil," a simile repeated in Song of Songs 1:3. Olive oil was also a symbol of joy, the "oil of gladness" of Psalm 45:7. The origins of anointing with oil (Ex. 30:30, Lev. 8:12, I Sam. 16:13, 1 Kgs. 1:39, Ps. 23:5) are not known, but we may speculate: olive oil rubbed on the skin was known as a remedy (Isa. 1:6, Luke 10:34) and it is possible that as the oil was observed absorbed into the skin with positive effects, it was hoped that kingly and priestly attributes would be "absorbed" into the anointed one in the same way. The word Messiah actually comes from the Hebrew word for anointing with oil.

Bitter, unprocessed olives served as a simile in the Babylonian Talmud, where the arguments between scholars were described as possessing "the bitterness of an olive."

But ever since the dove of Genesis 8:11 brought a "freshly plucked olive leaf" to Noah, and he therefore knew that the waters of the flood had receded, the olive leaf has become a worldwide symbol for peace and reconciliation.

CAKE MADE WITH OIL

"And from fine wheat flour, without yeast, make...cakes mixed with oil". (Ex. 29:2)

Not one biblical reference refers to actually eating olives! But other sources dating from the time of Jesus and shortly thereafter tell us that olives and olive oil were likely to have been part of every meal, from the tables of King David and Jesus to Ruth and Boaz's meal in the field. And a "cake made with oil" was one of the offerings to God in the Tabernacle and later in the Temple. We may assume that a similar dish was prepared in the family circle as well. Although the original "recipe" in Exodus does not mention honey, we found that a drizzle of sweetness enriches the dish and pleases the palate.

2 cups semolina   4 cups cold water   1/2 tsp. salt   1 cup olive oil   1/4 tsp. dried sage or 1 leaf per cake

Toast the semolina in a large ungreased pan, stirring constantly, for about 2-3 minutes. Place it in a bowl, and add the cold water and salt. Mix well. Return to pan and cook over a medium-high flame, stirring constantly, until the mixture thickens to the texture of a slightly dry porridge (about 7 minutes). Remove from the flame and allow to cool. Slowly pour in the olive oil, and continue mixing until it is well absorbed. Wet hands and form handfuls of the dough into round, plump cakes about the size of large oatmeal cookies. Placed on an ungreased pan and bake for 10-15 minutes in a medium oven.

Drizzle about half a teaspoon of honey on each cake after removing from the oven and before it completely cools.

$\bigcirc$ ther Fruits of the "Good Land"

"Pleasing to the Eye and Good for Food" (Gen. 2:9)

"...the fruits of the soil as an offering" (Gen. 4:3)

The Land of Israel, with its temperate climate, beneficial winter rains, and the rocky soil of its highlands, is conducive to orchard agriculture. "Do your best to bring back some of the fruit of the land", Moses instructed the spies he sent to explore Canaan (Num. 13:20). He knew that the sight of the fruit would be exotic and encouraging to the Israelites, who remembered Egypt much better for its vegetable gardens than for its orchards. The spies complied,

Fresh dates

and returned bearing not only the famously weighty cluster of grapes, but also pomegranates and figs. By the time of Jesus, over 30 kinds of fruit flourished in the country. The most important are among the Seven Species, of which we have already discussed wheat, barley, grapes, and olives. Dates, figs, and pomegranates were also on that list, and a closer look at them, as well as other fruits of the Land of the

The ancient Madaba Mosaic, depicting many Holy Land cities, shows Jericho, which the Bible called "the city of palms" (Deut. 34:3, Judg. 1:16 inter alia), surrounded by date palms.

Bible, brings us closer to the Bible verses and helps us better imagine what life was like in Bible days.

Dates

Dates are not specifically mentioned in the list of the Seven Species of the land of Israel. However the last item on that list, "honey," is the only one of the seven apparently not a fruit. But since date honey is mentioned often in ancient sources, it appears that the honey of the seven species is none other than the sweet thick juice of the date. Date honey was produced by boiling the dates in water, straining them through cloth, and continuing to cook the resulting liquid over a slow fire until reduced.

Clusters of ripe dates are ready for harvest by the end of the summer.

The origin of the scientific name for cultivated date, *phoenix dactylifera*, has an interesting tale to tell. The word phoenix may be connected to the coastal region of northern Canaan known as Phoenicia. The legendary eponymous ancient bird, known for having ended its life in a blaze, with its successor rising from the ashes, might have received its name from a similar characteristic that the date palm possesses - it is reborn, even after a fire, from shoots that spring from within its trunk. In Jewish and Christian tradition, the date palm symbolizes life, just as the phoenix did for other ancient cultures.

The source of the cultivated date is debatable, northeast Africa, Asia, Iraq or India. We do know that dates were first extensively cultivated in the low-lying region of southern Mesopotamia between the

A date orchard depicted in an ancient Egyptian tomb painting.

two ancient biblical rivers, the Tigris and the Euphrates, where they became the dominant fruit of the economy. The earliest human beings that we know of in the Bible Lands who ate dates lived at Telilat el-Ghassul in the southeastern Jordan Valley during the Chalcolithic period (4300-3500 BCE). People living around 3500 BCE left date pits in the cave known as the Cave of the Treasure at Nahal Mishmar, near the Dead Sea.

In the sixteenth century BCE, Pharaoh Thutmose III subdued a revolt of Canaanite cities under Egyptian domination (with biblical Megiddo/Armageddon at their head). In a wall painting in the Pharaoh's palace in Karnak in Egypt depicting his victory, dates are shown as one of the fruits of the defeated land. It has been suggested that Thutmose may have used his Canaan campaign to introduce some species of dates to Egypt that were previously unknown in his kingdom. A little over 3400 years later, the Egyptians may have "returned the favor": it is said that workers brought from Egypt to excavate Tel Megiddo brought dates with them - of a kind previously not grown in Palestine - as part of their food supply. The date pits they dropped took root, and can still be seen growing on the mound today.

The Bible notes that by the time the Children of Israel entered the Promised Land, dates were grown there:

A date plantation in the Jordan Valley.

when Moses looked across the land from Mount Nebo, he saw "...the plain of the Valley of Jericho, the city of palm trees, as far as Zoar " (Deut. 34:3). By the

Dates palms at Tel Megiddo National Park.

fourth century, dates were exported from the Land of Israel. The contemporary philosopher and botanist Theophrastus notes that dates from the Holy Land were particularly sought after because they were easy to preserve.

By the time of Jesus, the dates of Jericho (also called the city of palms in Judges 1:16, and 2 Chron. 28:15) were, together with balsam, the best-known products of this oasis city. It must have angered the Roman-era landlord of Jericho's date plantations, none other than the infamous Herod the Great, when, as historian Plutarch reports, Herod's friend Mark Anthony awarded the date plantations of Jericho to Cleopatra. She could not but have been pleased: not only were dates and date honey a tasty sweet, they also, "warm and satisfy, act as a laxative, and strengthen the body without spoiling it," reported the Babylonian Talmud Tractate *Ketuboth*. Date stones were fed to livestock and also used as fuel.

Josephus notes that dates were among the commodities stored up at Masada. Archaeological excavation proved the accuracy of this statement when excavators discovered date pits among the remains of food in Herod's opulent storehouses on the famous fortified plateau.

Cooking with Dates

"Pot-luck" in ancient times, says a commentary on the Babylonian Talmud's Tractate *Shabbat*, involved dates. If unexpected guests arrive, a man "takes what he finds in his house - walnuts and dates." Date gruel was a frequent dish, although not considered respectable for the Sabbath, because it did not keep well and might spoil. Dates were turned into even tastier treats by adding honey, walnuts, almonds, cinnamon, and even black pepper and cardamom.

The Symbolism of the Date Palm

The Roman conquerors of the Holy Land might have been the first to turn the date into a symbol of the land. They placed a date palm on a coin minted in honor of the quelling of the Great Revolt of the Jews against the Romans in 70 CE, on which the words *"Judaea capta"* were written and which depicted a woman sitting under the tree with a Roman soldier standing over her. In contrast, in Jewish and Christian tradition, because they grow near water, dates were a symbol of life - and of victory over death. When Jesus entered Jerusalem on the famed Sunday known as "Palm Sunday", John 12:13 says, "They took palm branches and went out to meet him."

Coins depicting date palms (132/3 CE)

What is the connection between date and life? In the dry climate of the Holy Land, the oasis was the all-important locale that could mean the difference between life and death for desert travelers. The towering date palm could be seen from a distance; it was the first sign that water was not far off, and therefore life was assured for parched and weary travelers. As a spiritual symbol of life, palms adorned the First Temple (I Kings 6:29) and they appear often in ancient synagogue decorations (and modern ones). They are mentioned extensively in Ezekiel 40, in the prophet's vision of the Temple. Psalm 92:12-15 also makes symbolic reference to the date: "The righteous will flourish like a palm tree, they will grow like a cedar of Lebanon; planted in the house of the Lord."

In a commentary on the book of Numbers, *Bamidmar Rabba*, Jewish sages note that some dates taste better when fresh, others, when stored. They then extrapolate from the culinary to the communal: "Thus too it is with Israel. Some were learned, some unversed in the law, and boorish, and just as there are soft dates that cannot be stored and others that bear fruit that can be kept safely, so was it with Israel, some entered the land and some did not."

The immature, still closed, sword-shaped leaf of the date palm, or frond, known in Hebrew as the *Lulav*, is one of the "Four Species" of the Feast of Tabernacles (Lev. 23:40). In seeking a reason for the selection of the date frond as one of the Four Species, the ancients pointed out that it resembles a human spine. From here it was not hard to see that the date palm, as a tree that is "upright", could also symbolize the desirable "upright" human character (S. of S. 7:8, Ps. 92:12).

The date is, as noted, very tall. Its height, explained the sages in a commentary on Genesis, *Midrash Rabba*, was also a reason to compare it to a righteous person: "As the hearts of palms and cedars point towards heaven, so does the heart of the righteous point towards the Holy One, blessed be He."

One kind of date palm had a negative connotation: because date palms do not grow well in the mountains, to call someone "a mountain palm" was tantamount to calling that person a fool.

A lintel from the fifth-century synagogue door at Capernaum. Date palms, like others of the biblical Seven Species, were among the first Jewish artistic themes.

And since only the best fruits were to be brought to the Temple, it is not surprising to find, in a commentary on the Mishnaic Tractate *Bikkurim*, dealing with the First Fruits, that mountain dates were excluded from the list of those fruits that could be brought to the Temple in fulfillment of the commandment of the First Fruits.

The Palm Sunday procession descending the Mount of Olives. Date palms, because they grow near life-giving water, became symbols of eternal life and hope.

Figs

The English word "fig" probably comes from the Hebrew word *paga*, which means an unripe fig. Though scientists tell us that figs may have their botanical origins in the Arabian Peninsula, no one can doubt their biblical origins: in the Garden of Eden, Adam and Eve covered their nakedness with fig leaves.

Outside of the Bible, the fig is first mentioned in Egyptian documents from about 2700 BCE, and later, in the third century BCE, as a fruit imported from the Holy Land to Egypt together with olives, nuts, honey, and pomegranates. Roman naturalist and historian Pliny tells of a tiny fig, *cottana* (perhaps from the Hebrew word *katan* - small) that was imported from Syria - a geographical designation that in Roman times also included Israel.

The fig, a member of the mulberry family, was available year-round, fresh in mid-summer around harvest time, dried to be eaten on journeys, or pressed and squeezed into a cake (1 Chr. 12:40). It was therefore considered inexpensive nourishment. The sugar in it was a quick source of energy, as noted in I Samuel 30:12: the Amalekite who reported the death of King Saul to David ate part of a cake of pressed figs and two

Fresh figs are a succulent biblical snack.

cakes of raisins, "and was revived." In the kitchen, stringed figs or single dried ones were put into cooking just like a spice. The fig also had medicinal uses. In Isaiah 38:21 it appears as a poultice given to King Hezekiah who was at death's door, apparently due to an infected boil. Modern research has shown that fig sap is an effective element in treating skin cancer.

The fig tree lent its name to two villages on the Mount of Olives, where the fruit was apparently particularly plentiful. Bethphage, or *Beit Pagi* (House of Unripe Figs) and Bethany - *Beit Te'enah*, the house of the fig. It was near Bethany that Jesus cursed the fig tree that had produced leaves but no fruit. This was not the usual situation; normally, the fig tree's leaves and its first fruit appear at the same time. The fig tree needed tending, as Proverbs 27:18 indicates: "He who tends a fig tree will eat its fruit, and he who looks after his master will be honored." We can understand this when we look more closely at the cultivation of the fig. In the wild, the fig tree remains a small bush, but when

cultivated can grow to a height of anywhere from 15-40 feet, especially near water. The well cared-for fig tree could therefore turn into a shade tree (John 1:48, Micah 4:4; Zech. 3:10). The fruit needs careful attention. Like the sycomore (see below), to ensure a good harvest, the farmer would pierce each young fig the way the fig wasp does (the piercing allows the fig to be fertilized). He would then cover it with oil, which apparently protected it from insect infestation.

Adam and Eve, from a thirteenth century French manuscript. The British Library, London.

Unlike other fruit trees, generally planted within fences, the fig was also planted outside of gardens. Passing strangers had access to it, so if the farmer did not guard it, he could lose his entire harvest (Isaiah 28:4 mentions a person who swallowed a fig "ripe before the harvest," i.e., took it before its owner could reach it). Because ripe figs spoil quickly, the farmer had to be at the ready to harvest any figs that were ripe, even rising at dawn. It is interesting that the special Hebrew word for harvesting figs is *oreh*, which refers to the light of dawn.

The fig tree was known not only for its fruit, "good and sweet," (Judg. 9:11) but also for its sap. As mentioned in the chapter on milk products, cheese could be curdled by adding fig sap. This was of interest to the ancient sages because of the prohibition against consuming fruit from trees less than three years of age (Lev. 19:23), with the fourth year's fruit a thanksgiving offering to God. The sages concluded that using the sap of the fruit would indeed be forbidden during this time, but use of the sap from the leaves and branches would be permitted.

The Fig as a Symbol

Jeremiah and Hosea both had visions of baskets of figs (Jer. 24: 2-8); the "good figs" - the elite of the nation, would be deported to Babylon, while the "bad figs", King Zedekiah and his officials, and the commoners, remained in Jerusalem. Hosea 9:10 saw the young nation of Israel as resembling the "early fruit on the fig tree." Destruction of the country's fig trees was a prophetic symbol of destruction of the land (Jer. 5:17,8:13, Hos. 2:12).

Teaching the disciples to read the signs of the times, Jesus used the fig tree as an example: "Now learn this lesson from the fig tree: as soon as its twigs get tender and its leaves come out, you know that summer is near" (Matt. 24:32-33).

A ripe fig with stem and leaves.

The farmer at rest after a long season of work might have been the inspiration for the image of tranquility represented by the fig tree and the grapevine in Solomon's day as described in I Kings 4:24-25: "During Solomon's lifetime Judah and Israel, from Dan to Beersheba, lived in safety, each man under his own vine and fig tree."

Pomegranates

A mosaic from the Church the Nativity in Bethlehem depicting pomegranates.

In color and form, the pomegranate may vie for the title of the most beautiful of all fruit in the Land of Israel. Its pleasing aspect made it an object for artistic imitation: pomegranates alternating with gold bells hung from the hem of the High Priest's robe (Ex. 28:33-34). They also decorated the capitals of the pillars that stood outside the doors of the Holy of Holies in the First Temple (1 Kgs. 7:18; 2 Chron. 3:16).

Pomegranates, usually crafted in silver, are still used as an adornment to modern Torah scrolls, a means of remembering the ancient Temple. The Hasmoneans, the Jewish dynasty that ruled the land of Israel from the mid-second and first centuries BCE, minted a coin on which a single pomegranate appeared, perhaps a reminder of the glories of Solomon's Temple. Later, three pomegranates appear together on coins of the rebels against Roman rule. Rinds of pomegranates were found in biblical Gezer, in remains of the city dating from the Bronze Age (3300-3050

The "Sycomore-Fig"

The sycomore fig is a relative of the domesticated fig (It is unconnected with the sycamore, the name by which the American plane tree and the English maple are sometimes called). In Amos 7:14 the prophet says he was a shepherd and also "took care of sycomore figs." The cultivation of this fruit involved climbing the tree to pierce it with an awl-like tool, while still unripe, to allow it to be fertilized and produce a better fruit. It was not unusual to see people occupied with this task up in the sycomore trees in the late summer. This is probably where vertically-challenged Zaccheus got the inspiration to climb this particular tree to get a better view of Jesus in Jericho (Luke 19:1-5).

Modern commentators have come across an interesting symbolic connection to Zaccheus' selection of the sycomore as a perch. The Hebrew name for the sycomore-fig is *shikma*, which comes from the same Hebrew word as "rehabilitate," because the sycomore can be restored from even the puniest remains of its trunk. This information can invest with new meaning Jesus' call to the tax collector to come down from the tree: it shows that even the life of a person so disparaged in those days can be renewed like the sycomore.

Pomegranates, a symbol of plenty, often appear on ancient coins. This coin was minted in Jerusalem in 67 CE.

BCE). In Numbers 20:5, the Israelites complained to Moses that he had brought them to a land that they feared lacked pomegranates, among other fruits. They must have been relieved to see that pomegranates were in fact among the fruits of Canaan, as they took stock of the produce that the spies brought back from their exploration of the land. Pomegranates had likely been available to the Egyptians since the invasion of the Hyksos (Semitic princes from Canaan or Syria) brought the fruit to Egypt in around 1600 BCE. An Egyptian papyrus from the thirteenth century BCE describes preparation for a reception held by the Pharaoh. On the menu were "beans, figs and pomegranates from Syria, and apples."

Pomegranates hang heavy on the tree by the end of summer in the Holy Land.

In ancient Egypt, a juice was made from the pomegranate that was considered an aphrodisiac; pomegranate wine was also manufactured. Pomegranates were eaten fresh, and, according to Roman food writer Columella, they were also pickled.

The pomegranate had other uses as well: the rind was a remedy for intestinal worms, the flowers were used to manufacture red dye, and the yellow inner rind for staining leather.

The pomegranate, like all of the Seven Species, flowers between Passover and Pentecost, and ripens towards the end of summer. It was therefore one of the fruits considered suitable to be brought to the Temple as an offering on the Feast of Tabernacles, which celebrates the fall harvest.

The large number of seeds in a ripe pomegranate figures in ancient sayings.

The pomegranate branch was used as a skewer for the lamb that was roasted in Jerusalem on Passover, because it is moisture-rich and was therefore not quickly consumed by the cooking fire.

The Symbolism of the Pomegranate

The beauty of the pomegranate was not lost on Solomon, who compared the temples of a beautiful woman "behind the veil" to two halves of a pomegranate (S. of S. 6:7). In the Song of Songs 6:11, spring was characterized by the budding of the pomegranates, whose distinctive flame-colored blossom was (and still is) outstanding among the seasonal flowers daubing the hillsides of Galilee and Judea. On the other hand, in Joel 1:12 and Haggai 2:19, the withering of the pomegranate, together with that of the other fruits of the Seven Species, symbolized Exile.

Specific aspects of the pomegranate's beautiful form evoked other positive images: the top of the pomegranate has the shape of a crown. Therefore, the pomegranate began to be associated with the Five Books of Moses, which was known also as "the crown of Torah". The numerous seeds of the pomegranate gave rise to an ancient expression originating in the Talmud: "as full of good deeds [or wisdom] as a pomegranate is full of seeds", an expression still in use today. In a commentary on the Song of Solomon, the sages compared school children sitting together in rows to the closely packed seeds of a pomegranate.

Portion of a mosaic from the sixth century mosaic of Beit Alfa, showing a pomegranate tree, birds, and fish.

Carobs

The carob is not mentioned *per se* in the Old Testament. However commentators deduce that one of its products was first mentioned in Genesis 43:11, in the list of gifts which Jacob sent to Egypt, under the guise of the last item on that list, "a little honey." It is assumed that this was probably carob honey, since bee's honey would have been common in Egypt, and therefore not an impressive offering. Experts say that, in fact, cultivation of the carob tree likely originated in the Holy Land, and from here the fruit made its way to Anatolia, and eventually to Greece, Italy, Egypt, and North Africa.

Buds of the carob blossoms.

The carob is the fruit of the tree known also as the boxer tree and, significantly for lovers of Bible lore, St. John's Bread. Mark 1:6 and Matthew 3:4 state that John the Baptist was nourished by "locusts and wild honey". Scholars have debated the nature of the "locust" mentioned here. According to Leviticus 11:22, John could have been eating grasshoppers, but most agree that John was actually eating the fruit of the locust tree, the carob.

Jewish tradition speaks of the carob in relation to Rabbi Simeon Bar Yohai, a rebel against Roman rule who lived in the early second century and was so high on the Roman "wanted list" that he had to hide out in a cave for many years. While in the cave, goes the legend, the rabbi was nourished solely on the fruit of a carob tree that miraculously grew within the cave, and a spring that never ran dry.

Immature carob pods. The one in the foreground is open, showing the seeds inside.

Modern science has proven what the ancients knew instinctively, that the carob is highly nutritional. Not only does it contain various vitamins, but gum from the ground carob seed (known to natural food experts as locust bean gum) containing the sugar compound known as arabinose, provides fiber that is essential to healthy digestion, by absorbing water and adding bulk to the large intestine. Because it was nutritious as well as easy to digest, the carob was made into porridge that was considered a healthy food for the elderly.

Carobs ripen in mid-summer. The trees had to be planted at some distance from each other because their roots would become entangled with each other and with other trees. Therefore, in the days of Jesus, a typical mountain farm might contain a grove of olives and grapes and a field of wheat or barley, interspersed with carob trees. The Talmudic tractate *Peah*, dealing with the gleanings for the poor, puts it this way, "Every carob tree has a clear view of its neighbor."

A carob tree flourishes in a Galilee field.

Once picked, the carob pod can be stored and was available year-round in large quantities. It was therefore a significant part of the diet of poor people. In 2 Kings 6:25, which describes the siege on Samaria by the Assyrians, hardship was so great that, "a donkey's head sold for eighty shekels of silver, and a quarter of a cab of seedpods for five shekels". The seedpods in question were probably the carob, as the text wanted to show the inflated price for the lowest - and least desirable - food product.

The fact that the carob was not considered a desirable food is also mentioned by inference in the story of the Prodigal Son. In Luke 15:16 it says, "He longed to fill his stomach with the pods that the pigs were eating."

The carob had non-food uses as well. Carob leaves contain a high quantity of tannin and so were in demand in the ancient tanning industry. A golden color was extracted from the green pods. Locust bean gum was also made into a glue in the traditional villages of the Holy Land until relatively recently.

The seeds contained within the carob pod are so similar to each other that they could be used as a standard weight, the *gerah* in Hebrew. The biblical half-shekel, given as a donation to the sanctuary and later to the Temple and first mentioned in Exodus 30:13, weighed 20 *gerahs*. Through the Greek name for the carob seed, *keration*, we have gained the English word for the weight known as a carat, equal today to about 200 milligrams.

The Carob as a Symbol

A little known translation of Isaiah 1:19-20 brings us from carob as poor people's fare to carob as a symbol of privation. The usual translation reads "If you are willing and obedient, you will eat the best from the land; but if you resist and rebel you will be devoured by the sword." A more accurate reading of the verse results in the translation "you will devour the carob." The words for "sword" and "carob" are almost identical in Hebrew and clearly related, perhaps because of the scimitar-shape of the carob's seedpod. The association between the carob and privation is also noted in an ancient Midrash, or homily, written in the wake of the Temple's destruction and the period of ensuing want in the land. "A Jew has to suffer anguish and privation to the point of a menu exclusively of carobs, and only then does he accept the rule of God and repent..."

The Citron

A citron.

The citron, which may be the origin of all citrus fruit, is thought to have originated in India. It is interesting that by its Hebrew name, *etrog*, the citron is nowhere mentioned in the Old Testament. Yet, for at least the last two thousand years it has been thought of as a biblical fruit, and it is essential to the celebration of the Feast of Tabernacles.

The citron's centrality is due to its identification by the sages of the time of Jesus as the otherwise-unnamed "choice fruit from the trees" of Leviticus 23:40. Better known as "boughs of goodly trees" in the King James version of the Bible, this fruit, together with palms, willows, and "thick trees" (later identified with myrtle), were to be brought before God in rejoicing. How did the sages come to their conclusions regarding the identity of the "goodly tree"? Here is one of the most interesting of the discussions on the matter, taken from the Jerusalem Talmud, Tractate *Succah*: "What is this fruit of the [goodly] tree of loveliness that its fruit is beauty and itself is beauty. It is the etrog. Could it not be the pomegranate? No, for though its fruit be lovely, not so the tree. Could it be the carob? No, for though the tree be lovely, not so the fruit. But where fruit and tree alike are beauty - that is the etrog alone."

Many other sources point to the beauty of both the wood of the tree and the fruit. The wood was much in demand, as shown by the list in Revelation 18:12 of valuable items in the market that would be no longer available after the destruction of Babylon.

The fruit was served fresh, especially to children, and was eaten pickled and boiled. The citron had many medicinal uses. Its fruit or seed, soaked in wine, was an antidote to poison. It was forbidden to keep milk or wine uncovered lest a snake creep in. If that should occur, says Tractate *Shabbat* of the Babylonian Talmud, one must take a whole etrog, cut out the inside, fill it with honey, put it on burning coals, and eat it. The citron was also in demand as a breath freshener, and its seeds were recommended for women suffering from morning sickness.

In the time of Jesus, the citron was cultivated in the Jordan Valley, as well as in Judea and Samaria. One of the famed letters sent by Bar Kochba, commander of the Second Revolt of the Jews against the Romans, instructs his subordinates to send citrons to the rebel camp from Ein

Worshippers hold the Four Species during Feast of Tabernacles prayers at the Western Wall.

Gedi near the Dead Sea, so that the Festival of Succoth (Tabernacles) could be properly observed.

The Symbolism of the Citron

A Guiness Record: The largest citron ever grown, at Neot Kedumim Biblical Landscape Reserve.

Because ripe citrons can be found hanging on the tree virtually year-round, they became a symbol of fertility. The "nipple" of the citron (the protuberance from which the flower was attached) was the part of the fruit most associated with fertility, and at the time of Jesus was much in demand as a cure for barrenness and to encourage the birth of a boy.

Walnuts

The popularity of the walnut, first brought to the Land of Israel from Persia, derived from its myriad uses, including oil for lighting, cooking, eating the nut itself, and the outer husk as a source of dye. The Greeks called it "Royal Persian" reflecting its Persian origin as stated, and its kingly attributes that also spilled over into its full Hebrew name, *egoz melech* - "king's nut."

The "grove of nut trees" mentioned in the Song of Solomon 6:11 was a walnut grove. Significantly, the narrator goes down to the grove. In fact, walnuts were planted at low points in the valleys so that they could get a good dose of frost in winter, which they needed to develop properly.

The Symbolism of the Walnut

Walnuts are not mentioned specifically in the New Testament, but in the Talmud, which is, as noted, an accurate reflection of New Testament times, they are frequently mentioned. The fusion between their husk and meat, for example, became a symbol of the harmony of marriage. Therefore, we may imagine that in the bridal procession of the "ten virgins" (Matt 25:1), walnuts were cast playfully among the torch-bearers.

A walnut has burst its outer skin and is ready for harvest.

Almonds

The Hebrew word for almond, *shaked*, comes from the root word for diligence, or "watching" as Jeremiah 1:12 puts it. Knowing this, we can better appreciate what was meant by Jeremiah 1:11-12. "The word of the Lord came to me: 'What do you see, Jeremiah? ' 'I see the branch of an almond tree,' I replied. The Lord said to me, 'You have seen correctly, for I am watching [or, as some translations have it, "hastening"] to see that my word is fulfilled.'"

The almond indeed diligently watches for the passing of the height of winter. It is the first tree to blossom in early spring, painting the hillsides of Judea and Galilee in pastels of pink and cream. Its beauty lent itself to ancient artistic representation, its "buds and blossoms" (Ex. 25:33 *inter alia*) becoming the model for the joints between segments of the Menorah, the candelabra that was in the Tabernacle and later in the Temple.

The sages around the time of Jesus made mention of the almond's many assets: it produces a delicious almond paste, a relish, oil, and was considered excellent as an ingredient in cooking. Though some almonds were bitter, these could be made tasty by cooking them in water. Almond husks were used as fuel.

Blossoming almonds dot the landscape of Israel in late winter.

The cultivated apple arrived in the Holy Land, perhaps from Persia, about four thousand years ago. It was a fruit widely enough grown to lend its name - *tapuach* in Hebrew - to certain places in the land. Joshua conquers the king of Tappuah (Josh. 12:17), and later in Joshua 17:7 we read about "En Tappuah" (the Spring of Tappuah) and that Manasseh had the land of Tappuah, but Tappuah itself, on the boundary of Manasseh, belonged to the Ephraimites (Josh. 17:8).

In the days of the prophet Joel (the early ninth century BCE) the apple had become an important enough element in the economy of Judah to be included among better-known biblical fruits. In bewailing the future destruction of the land in terms of the damage done by a swarm of locusts (a much-feared blight of farmers in Bible days): "The vine is dried up and the fig tree is withered; the pomegranate, the palm and the apple tree - all the trees of the field - are dried up" (Joel 1:11).

The Symbolism of the Almond

As mentioned, the almond's early blossoming made it a symbol for vigor. In Numbers 17, the story is told that Moses created staffs for the heads of the tribes, and each staff was planted at the entrance to the Tabernacle. The staff of Aaron was the only one that budded, producing almonds. Here, once again, the almond is a symbol of vigor. In Ecclesiastes, conversely, the almond symbolizes old age, because of its white blossoms, reminiscent in this case of white hair of old age, "when men are afraid of heights, and of dangers in the streets; when the almond tree blossoms, and the grasshopper drags himself along, and desire no longer is stirred, then man goes to his eternal home and mourners go about the streets" (Eccl 12:5).

Also On the Biblical Table

From various ancient sources, we are aware that many fruits were eaten that are not mentioned in the Bible. Since they could have been part of any New Testament-era meal, let us consider peaches, apples, plums, and apricots.

Peach trees were planted in or near vineyards, a fact that we know from the talmudic account of a certain disgruntled peach-grower who sued his neighbor because his neighbor's grapevine had so grown over his own peach tree as to split it apart! The judges in this case required the vine-grower to provide his neighbor with a new peach tree. There are also some references to apricots in the region of the Holy Land from about the second century BCE. The pear is another fruit that was apparently plentiful around the time of Jesus, a fact that we can deduce from its frequent appearance in rabbinic discussions regarding tithes and other issues.

Because of the attributes of the "apple" as they appear in the Song of Songs in 2:3, 2:5, and 7:8, scholars debate whether it is the same species of fruit that we call the apple today, the same as the fruit described by Pliny and other ancient naturalists as growing in this region.

The phrase "apple of the eye" appears in the English translation of the Bible in Deuteronomy 2:8, and Psalm 17:8. That the phrase indicates a prized possession is clear. However, we cannot deduce this from the original Hebrew where the word translated into English as "apple" is not *tapuach*, but rather *ishon*, the pupil of the eye, the most precious part of the eye.

In the days of Jesus, applesauce, and apple cider were among the foods made out of apples. Grated apple added to porridge was said to improve its flavor. Apples were mashed and added to dough to act as yeast and cause the dough to rise.

On the mosaic floor of the Roman villa at Sepphoris, summer is depicted as a woman holding a basket of ripe summer fruit.

The Caper

Not everyone knows that the salty little round delicacy they spoon out of a jar to add flavor to their salads was well-known at the time of Jesus as a plant growing wild

The caper flower.

in rocky places - from that day to this - from the Galilee to the Judean desert and the Negev. Like today, its edible flower buds were pickled in salt or vinegar and considered a delicacy. The buds had to be picked precisely at the right moment in their lives to be tastily prepared, and cultivation of the caper bush was a job for an expert. Elazar, a talmudic rabbi who lived in the Golan Heights, was such an expert, as a stone inscription discovered on the site of his ancient study house notes. The immature fruit of the caper bush were also pickled and eaten.

Aspects of the caper also became symbolic. Because it grows so tenaciously among the rocks, the "caper among the shrubs" became a symbol of the Jewish People's will to survive, as mentioned in the Talmudic Tractate *Beitza*. A mistranslation of most English renditions of Ecclesiastes 12:5 has lost the opportunity to consider the significance of the fact that the caper blossoms quickly and almost immediately scatters its seeds. True to the Hebrew original, that verse should read: "The almond tree may blossom, the grasshopper be burdened, and the caper bush may bud again, but man sets out for his eternal abode..."

The Forbidden Fruit" of the Garden of Eden

There is no hint in the text of Genesis 2:17, which mentions "the tree of the knowledge of good and evil" as to what the fruit of that tree might have been. The origins of the representation of the fruit as an apple are ancient, but shrouded in mystery. Nearly two thousand years ago, Jewish sages discussed the mysterious identity of the forbidden fruit in symbolic terms. Perhaps, they offered among other suggestions, it might have been the carob, for carob comes from a Hebrew root word meaning destruction.

The Babylonian Talmud and various legends indicate that the tree of knowledge was the fig tree. Rashi says it has to do with the fact that they used fig leaves to cover themselves: "...which they had eaten, and by the very thing by which they were corrupted they were rectified." In Latin, the word *peccare*, "to sin", is associated with the Hebrew word *"pag"* (unripe fig). Some commentators have deduced that the "tree of the knowledge of good and evil" (Gen. 2:9) was the fig tree, because it was obviously nearest them when they discovered they were naked.

Adam and Eve in the Garden of Eden, by Oleg Trabish

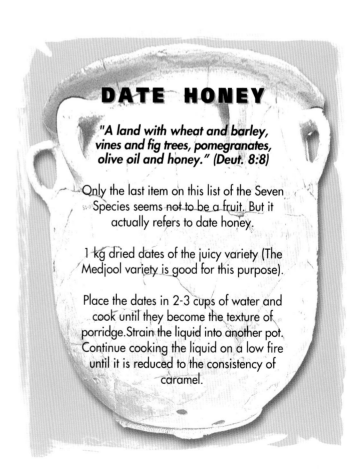

DATE HONEY

"A land with wheat and barley, vines and fig trees, pomegranates, olive oil and honey." (Deut. 8:8)

Only the last item on this list of the Seven Species seems not to be a fruit. But it actually refers to date honey.

1 kg dried dates of the juicy variety (The Medjool variety is good for this purpose).

Place the dates in 2-3 cups of water and cook until they become the texture of porridge. Strain the liquid into another pot. Continue cooking the liquid on a low fire until it is reduced to the consistency of caramel.

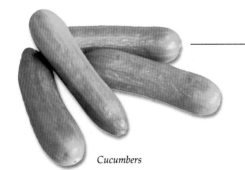

$\mathcal{V}$egetables

"Every green plant for food" (Gen. 1:30)

Cucumbers

Although the idea of paradise as a flourishing garden has persisted over the generations in art and literature as the epitome of plenty and peace, vegetables were not high on the list of preferred foodstuffs. The above quotation expresses this attitude. The rather lowly place of vegetables comes to us from a later source as well, the Babylonian Talmud, which states, "If a man goes to stay at a person's house, on the first day he will receive chickens, on the second day fish, on the third day meat, on the fourth day lentils, and so on down until he is fed vegetables." (It is interesting that chicken, because of its rarity at the time of Jesus and until the fourth century appears on this list ahead of red meat, not the case in our day.)

Vegetables - "cucumbers, melons, leeks, onions, and garlic" do have a prominent place on the list of items the Israelites missed from Egypt (Numbers 11: 5). They also win honorable mention in Daniel 2:8-15, where they had a more salubrious effect on Daniel and the other young men brought to the king's household (Daniel 1:8-15) than the "choice food and wine" of the royal table. In the decades close to the time of Jesus, vegetables were an important enough component of ancient diets that the Babylonian Talmud states, "It is forbidden to live in a city where there is no vegetable garden."

Imagine making a meal, especially a Mediterranean one, without tomatoes, eggplants, green or red peppers, and potatoes. Our biblical ancestors in fact knew nothing of

these vegetables; they arrived on the scene much later from the New World. Moreover, cucumbers as we know them today, had not reached Mediterranean shores in Scripture days, and the biblical cucumber was more like what we call zucchini.

Classes of Grasses

A distinction was made between garden vegetables and field, or wild, vegetables, or "herbs", in the language of Scripture. Among wild vegetables were various kinds of greens that might be looked down upon today as mere grass or weeds. These included mallows, and two sorts of other greens, orach, and rocket. (During the 1948 War of Independence, when Jerusalem was besieged, many of the inhabitants staved off hunger by collecting mallows.) Some scholars see the "tasteless food" of Job 6:6, *hallamit* in Hebrew, as mallows.

The flowering mallow plant.

In the Bible, this class of quickly growing, but just as quickly withering "grasses," served as a symbol of mortality (Ps. 37:2, Ps. 90:5 *inter alia*).

Orach, known in the Book of Job as "saltwort" (Job 30:4), is a prolific bush that normally grows in desert areas, and exudes a large amount of salt on its leaves, making it an important component for salt-replacement in the diet of desert animals. A saltwort patch has been discovered growing in Jerusalem near the grounds of an ancient church, which may indicate that it was transplanted there and cultivated.

The Israelites certainly rejoiced over their liberation from Egypt, but Numbers 11:5 says that they also complained that they missed the onions they had enjoyed in the land of their bondage.

Saltwort.

Scallions are native to the southern coast of the Holy Land.

Various wild greens served as the "bitter herbs" to be served with the Pascal Lamb (Ex. 12:8). Ancient commentators defined several wild growing greens as suitable for use as the bitter herb. Among them are chicory, and a member of the Umbelliferae family known as sea holly in English.

The sages noted that these plants were sweet tasting at the beginning of their growing season in the winter, but by Passover had attained the bitter taste that qualified them for Passover use. In their minds, this was symbolic of the Israelites' stay in Egypt, which at first was sweet, but eventually became embittered by slavery.

Centaury

From the numerous mentions of vegetables and vegetable dishes in sources contemporary with the time of Jesus, we can be certain that they were on every table at which Jesus reclined for a meal. However vegetables, as such, are mentioned only once in the New Testament, in Romans 14:2. Here, Paul discusses the dietary decisions faced by new Christians, some of whom, in order to avoid eating meat prepared for idol worship (an important principle in Jewish dietary laws) abstained from meat entirely and ate only vegetables.

Other Vegetables

Among "garden vegetables" at the time of Jesus, Luke 11:42 mentions "mint, rue, and all other kinds of garden herbs".

Beets (though once again, not the same species we know today) were on the menu, and although they were considered a poor man's food, it was said that their flavor improved when cooked with meat. Spring onion is indigenous to this part of the world. It was imported to Europe by the Crusaders in the Middle Ages, who found it growing near the old Philistine city of Ashkelon, and named it escallion, from which derives the other name for the spring onion, scallion.

The healthful properties of garlic were first recognized in ancient times.

Garlic was a common food. The Jews had such a fondness for this pungent vegetable that in Roman writings, and in the Mishna, they were known ethnically as "eaters of garlic." The Talmud refers to the seasoning of numerous dishes with garlic, and recommended it as an aphrodisiac.

In Joshua 15:37, a place in the western foothills of Judea, called Dilean, is mentioned. Looking at the root of this word, linguists recognize the Hebrew for gourd, indicating that this vegetable, probably the bottle gourd, was also grown in the area. A species of gourd (though not the pumpkin or squash we know of today) has long been cultivated in the ancient Near East; seeds were discovered in Egyptian tombs from about 3000 BCE. Interestingly, scholars suggest that the gourd was first cultivated not as food but as a container for liquids and seeds!

In 2 Kings 4:39-40, we discover that Elisha the prophet knew a gourd-based recipe involving flour. The exact identity of the "wild vine" or the "gourd" that was picked and put in the pot, and why the prophets saw "death in the pot" is debated. One opinion has identified it as a species of poisonous watermelon known to botanists as *Citrullus colocythis*. It is a cathartic, which might account for the uneasiness of diners "as they began to eat" (2 Kings 4:40).

Biblical terrace agriculture has been recreated at Sataf in the Judean Mountains.

"Irrigated by Foot"

The fertility of Egypt depended entirely on a supply of water brought from the Nile. It was a land where vegetables thrived, as can be gleaned from that list of products that the recalcitrant Children of Israel missed in the desert (Num. 11:5). Everything on this list was apparently grown in the neighboring Land of Israel (although as mentioned, not always the same species we know today). In Egypt, vegetables had to be watered by constructing water channels through the field, pumping up water from the Nile and constantly patrolling the vegetable patches to make sure the channels remained unclogged. If it appeared that one patch was getting more water than another, the farmer could put his foot in the channel to divert the water elsewhere. This is likely to be the meaning behind the verse, "the land you are entering to take over is not like the land of Egypt, from which you have come, where you planted your seed and irrigated it by foot as in a vegetable garden" (Deut 11:10-11).

Even though the Land of Israel depended on rainfall rather than irrigation, here too, the Children of Israel channeled water to grow vegetables alongside orchards of fruit trees, in the cultivation of which the land of Israel excelled over Egypt. The vegetable patches in the Holy Land, however, had to be planted atop the large, flat slabs of limestone that characterize its mountain slopes. These are natural terraces that became stepped vegetable patches when the farmers built low stone walls following the curves of the hills, leveling the area with soil. Approximately 60 percent of the hills west of Jerusalem are terraced even today, with

some ancient terraces going back to the settlement period of Joshua.

Winter rains pelted field and orchard in the Holy Land providing its greatest benefit by replenishing mountain springs, which had slowed to a trickle over seven to eight rainless months. This was the water that the biblical farmer directed into his vegetable patches. Proverbs describes God's control even over kings, depicting God as a farmer maintaining his watercourses: "The king's heart is in the hand of the Lord; he directs it like a watercourse wherever he pleases" (Prov. 21:1). The ancient farmer in Judea increased his supply of available spring water by digging a channel into the mountain itself, widening the water bearing layer and allowing a greater volume of water to flow out of the spring into pools he had prepared, from

Intensively maintained water channels for irrigation have been used in Egypt from Bible times to the present.

which channels would lead to the terraces. This may be the origin of the beautiful simile of the Song of Solomon 4:12: "You are a garden locked up, my sister, my bride; you are a spring enclosed, a sealed fountain."

Legumes

Both in Old Testament times and at the time of Jesus, legumes, the most famous of which

Lenti

were lentils, seem to have been the second most important component of diet after grain. We deduce this from a fascinating list, provided in the Mishna, of products with

Green and brown lentils.

which a man would have to supply his estranged wife each week. In addition to oil, dried figs, and approximately seven pounds of wheat in today's weight, a little less than two pounds of lentils was obviously considered essential. One ancient authority numbers over twenty kinds of legumes, among the most important of which were lentils and chickpeas.

Lentils are contained in the seedpods of a small annual plant with flowers that are white and violet striped. Not only can they be eaten fresh, but when dried they can be stored, making them invaluable to the ancient kitchen. Lentils were very common in Syria and Egypt, especially the red variety. Some scholars say that the biblical land of Edom (whose rocks and soil are of a rust-red hue and whose name comes from the Hebrew word for "red") got its name from the red lentils that grew in profusion there. The most famous Biblical story concerning lentils is, of course, the red lentil stew for which Esau sold his birthright: "Then Jacob gave Esau some bread and some lentil stew. He ate and drank, and then got up and left... " (Gen 25:34).

Because dried and cooked lentils were preferred portable provisions for a journey, Barzillai brought them to David's hungry followers (2 Sam 17:28). The protein content in lentils made it a dish both nourishing and satisfying, especially when combined with grain. It is believed that the word "lent" may derive from the word lentil, as it became the custom to refrain from eating meat during this time, supplanting it with other nourishing food sources. Its nourishing qualities, the ease with which it can be stored and carried, made lentils typical farmer's fare. At the time of Jesus, one kind of lentil stew was made with onions.

Sweets were also prepared with lentils at the time of Jesus! In English, the beautiful verse of the Songs of Songs 2:5 "strengthen me with raisins, refresh me with apples," was a source of consternation to the ancient sages who lived around the time of Jesus. The Hebrew word used here, *ashashiyot*, is not raisins at all, although it was obvious from the context it was sweet. We cannot know if the ancient rabbis were working up an appetite for dessert when they discussed this subject, but one of them states that in his opinion, *ashashiyot* were "toasted lentils, ground, rolled in honey and fried".

Like many other biblical foods, lentils had many symbolic meanings. The sages noted the proximity in Scripture of the death of Abraham to the story of the selling of Jacob's birthright and deduced that Jacob was cooking the lentil stew as the "mourners' meal" (a meal cooked to both comfort and nourish a mourner) for his father Isaac after Abraham's passing. They also imagined that Adam and Eve ate lentils after the death of Abel. The connection between lentils and mourning in the minds of the rabbis was due to its round shape: "as the lentil rolls," they concluded in a commentary on Genesis, "so do death, sorrow, and mourning constantly roll about among men."

Another type of legume, chickpeas, was also typical farmer's fare in Bible days, as it is today. It was a common enough dish among the simple folk for Isaiah to use it in drawing a verbal picture of the wonders of the End of Days. In the original Hebrew, Isaiah speaks of chickpeas so plentiful that even the animals will eat them (although translators from ages past were not familiar with this legume, and so called it "fodder and mash!"): "...people of Zion, who live in Jerusalem, you will weep no more. How gracious he will be when you cry for help... He will also send you rain for the seed you sow in the ground, and the food that comes from the land will be rich and plentiful. In that day your cattle will graze in broad meadows. The oxen and donkeys that work the soil will eat fodder and mash, spread out with fork and shovel" (Isa. 30:19-24).

Fava beans, also known as horse beans or broad beans.

The Bible also mentions other kinds of legumes. The bread recipe in Ezekiel 4:9, mentions, together with other ingredients, "beans" which were to be ground. This word actually referred to a specific type of large, flat, tan-colored lentil with a black margin around it called *ful*, sometimes translated as horse bean, broad bean, or fava bean. *Ful* is still a regional favorite especially in Egypt where, as a stew (after cooking for 15 hours), it is considered breakfast food. It is a popular Egyptian street food too - sold on an open cart with lemon, cumin and *"aish"* bread. *Ful* can also replace chickpeas in felafel. Even though Ezekiel's recipe contains many ingredients, it was considered the bread of the poor, which Ezekiel was to bake as part of God's plan that the prophet should graphically demonstrate to the people the hardships of the exile that awaited them. In the days of Jesus, a popular recipe for the broad bean was to cut it in half, and cook it together with garlic, oil, and vinegar.

A Legume Legend From the Talmud

A variety of lentils are among the food products in this market display.

"This is the story of the slaves of King David who were sitting at a meal and eating eggs. One of them was very hungry and ate his portion before his friends did. He was then embarrassed because he had nothing before him. He said to the companion next to him, "lend me one egg." The companion said to him, "I will not lend you the egg until you swear to me in front of witnesses that you will give me all the profit that a man can attain from one egg for the time I lend it to you until I ask for the loan back." The hungry man agreed and the egg was given him before witnesses. After a long time the lender came to take back what was borrowed. When the borrower said, "I only owe you one egg," a dispute developed. Accordingly, they went before King David [for justice]. The king calculated that in one year one chick could be born from the egg, in the second year the chick could mother up to 18 chicks, in the third year the 18 could each mother 18 more, and so on until a huge sum accumulated. The borrower left the audience hall in a depression.

Solomon saw him and said, 'What did the king say?' The distressed man said, "The king said I owe a huge sum." Solomon said, "go and buy broad beans and cook them. And some day when the king wants to go somewhere, stand in the road he is to pass. At whatever time the king's

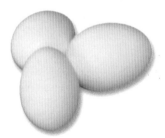

Hard boiled eggs and fava beans make a nutritious meal

guard passes by, sow the cooked broad beans in a plowed field on the way. Anyone who asks you what you are sowing, tell him 'I am sowing cooked broad beans.' And if he says, 'whoever saw anyone sowing cooked broad beans?' Answer him, 'and whoever saw a cooked egg produce a chick?'" Sure enough, when the king's guard passed by and asked him what he was sowing, he told them. When they responded in amazement, just as Solomon said they would, he had his chance to recite his prepared line: "And whoever heard of a cooked egg producing a chick?" Thus the word spread back through the ranks until it reached King David himself. King David went to the man and demanded, "Who told you to do this thing?" ...the

man admitted, "Solomon told me to do it, from start to finish." King David then changed his ruling and ordered the borrower to pay back exactly one egg to the lender. That is why it was said, 'O God, endow the king with your judgments, the king's son with your righteousness (Psalm 72:1).'"

Roses

"Gather Ye Rosebuds" - And Bring Them to the Kitchen

In a commentary on Ecclesiastes, one ancient source notes, "Never did the rose quit the table of Solomon." The rabbi who made this statement did not mean floral arrangements - he knew that the rose could produce a tasty dish. The Greeks made jam out of it, first picking the most fragrant flowers early in the morning, washing and drying them. Water was added as well as sugar or honey. Apicius made a powder of the petals and used it to add to soup or baked meats or fish. They also added crushed petals to salads. Fish and fowl broiled with rose hips were used in cooking. Rose water was used to dilute pomegranate juice and as a refreshing flavoring for water.

ELISHA'S GOURD STEW

The prophets of Gilgal found Elisha's version of this stew somewhat less than tasty. We cannot know exactly what species of gourd was used in Elisha's recipe, so we will rely on the familiar (but modern) gourd, pumpkin. 2 Kings 4:38 notes that there was a famine at that time, so we have selected only vegetables that would be growing during a Holy Land spring following a rainless winter.

1 cup pumpkin
1 onion
1-2 pressed cloves of garlic
wild asparagus (feel free to use the store-bought kind)
1 leek, sliced into 2 inch pieces
1/2 cup chopped chard (or spinach)
1/2 cup chopped mallows
1 sprig of hyssop or 1/2 tsp dried hyssop
1/2 tsp cumin
water to cover

Cook the vegetables until soft. Take 1 cup of the cooking water and mix it with 2 tbsps of flour until the mixture is smooth. Return it to the pot and continue to cook while stirring until the mixture thickens.

$\mathcal{F}$ish and other Fruit of the Ancient Sea

"Two Small Fish" (John 6:9)

> *Simon-Peter climbed aboard and dragged the net ashore. It was full of large fish, one hundred and fifty-three, but even with so many the net was not torn. Jesus said to them, "Come and have breakfast". (John 21:11-12)*

Anchors from the time of Jesus.

The fishermen disciples of Jesus could take pride in a profession extending as far back as the arrival of the Twelve Tribes into the Land of Israel: Zebulon's tribal inheritance included a portion of the Mediterranean coast near Mount Carmel. His brother Naphtali settled near the shores of the Sea of Galilee and ancient legends ascribe fishing skills to both.

The fishing prowess of Zebulon and Naphtali notwithstanding, the Bible also refers to fish imported from outside the boundaries of the Holy Land. The prophet Nehemiah (13:16) castigates the Jerusalemites of his day for buying fish on the Sabbath day, that had been brought to the markets of the Holy City by the Phoenicians from the port of Tyre (on the coast of the Mediterranean in modern-day Lebanon). There was even a special gate in Jerusalem called "the fish gate" (also mentioned in Nehemiah 3:3; 12:39 and Zephaniah 1:10), probably the closest Jerusalem gate to the local fish market. In the second century CE, the import of fish via the Mediterranean port of Acre was so common that rabbis, retelling the story of Moses turning his rod into a snake, put these words in the mouth of Pharaoh who disparaged the miracle: "that is as easy as bringing fish to Acre."

Fish were abundant in the Nile River, as the Bible tells us in Exodus 7:18. The Israelites particularly bemoan the absence of this component of their diet after they left Egypt (Num. 11:5). Over two millennia later, in the prophecies of Isaiah, we still find fish an important food in Egypt, one which the prophet predicted would be lost when Egypt paid the price of its idolatry: "The fishermen will groan and lament, all who cast hooks into the Nile; those who throw nets on the water will pine away." (Is.19:8)

In the Bible, fish appear as a symbol of fertility, life, and renewal (Ezek. 47:9-10). Due to the fertility of fish and their resulting abundance, an ancient cult developed around them. Moses included the likeness of a fish in the list of creatures he specifically warned the people of Israel against worshipping (Deut 4:18). In its form as a fish god, Dagon was revered by the coast-dwelling Phoenicians, who discovered this deity, "imported" from Mesopotamia, when they settled on the coast of Canaan in the thirteenth century BCE.

Detail of a mosaic from Sepphoris: a fisherman returns with his catch.

The strong link between food and religious worship is reflected once again in what may have been a "migration" of significance between Dagon of Mesopotamia and Dagon of the Philistines: In Mesopotamia, Dagon was a deity connected to grain and rain. It is possible that its significance was transformed to a fish-god by the Philistines because of the special interest this coastal-dwelling, sea-faring people would have had in creatures of the deep. The Philistines sometimes depicted Dagon as a half woman half fish, which may have been the source of the mermaid legend. As the primary deity in the pantheon of the Philistines, who were one of the more significant enemies of the Israelites, Dagon appears several times in the Bible, most notably in the story of the capture of the Ark of the Covenant in I Samuel 5.

Fishing in the Sea of Galilee

Due to the obvious difficulty in keeping fish fresh during transport, they do not appear to have been a significant component of the ancient Holy Land diet, except for people living near bodies of water. Around the Sea of Galilee, however, fish and fishing were naturally an important part of people's lives.

A mosaic discovered in Magdala on the Sea of Galilee depicts an ancient boat.

Several Gospel references allow us to infer that Peter ran an entire fishing business (Luke 5:7, Mark 1:20. John 21:1-3; Luke 5:11). Bethsaida, the hometown of at least three of the disciples, Philip, Andrew, and Peter, underwent a population explosion during the lifetime of its ruler Herod Philip, with a concomitant rise in the demand for fish, so Peter would have made a good living. Commentators note that in a fisherman's "job description" are the makings of a good apostle. Teamwork was required to operate the dragnet, likely to have been the type mentioned in Matthew 13:47 as a simile of the kingdom of heaven. Patience, strength, and fearlessness was part of using the cast net, operated by an individual fisherman, and likely to have been the kind wielded by Peter and Andrew in Matthew 4:20.

The Gospels mention fish several times as a component in meals, in fact more than they mention meat. In the Sermon on the Mount Jesus asks "...Which of you, if his son asks for bread, will give him a stone? Or if he asks for a fish, will give him a snake?" (Matt. 7:9-10). When Jesus' disciples gather, they have bread and fish for sustenance (Mark 6:37; 8:7).

Fish were eaten fresh by grilling or frying them, especially close to the lake itself, as in the story of the miraculous catch of fish in John 21. Early-rising visitors to the Sea of Galilee can to this day watch fishermen grilling or frying a portion of their fresh catch of the night before on the lakeshore or even right in their boat.

The trammel net was a three-layered net in which fish were trapped in the layers of mesh. It was piled into a boat and slipped into the sea.

If fish were to be carried on a journey, they would be dried and salted to preserve them. The Greek name for Magdala, the lakeside home of Mary Magdalene, was Taricheae, a word that comes from the Greek word for preserving. This was probably a central location for fish processing. In those days salting was basically the same as it is today: Fish were gutted, rubbed with coarse salt and left covered with alternating layers of salt and reed mats for 3-5 days. Then they were hung to dry further in the air. Sardines, the most plentiful fish in the Sea of Galilee from that day to this, would have to be salted in order not to waste them, especially because as many as ten tons of sardines could be caught in one night at the height of the sardine fishing season in early spring.

The dragnet was one of three types of nets used in the time of Jesus by fishermen on the Sea of Galilee. It was the longest and heaviest and required a large boat to maneuver it into place. Matthew 13:47 likens the kingdom of heaven to the dragnet "that was cast into the sea and gathered some of every kind".

The famous Galilee Boat, dating from the time of Jesus, was discovered mired in the mud on the Sea of Galilee shores and is now on display at Ginnosar in Galilee.

The Romans also bred fish; they harvested fertilized eggs and placed them in special lakes called *vivaria*. They sold the resulting young fish for stocking fishponds. By the Byzantine period, raising fish in artificial ponds was widespread in the Holy Land, as demonstrated by the remains of numerous quarried pools on the Coastal Plain of Israel.

Hook, Line, and Sinker

"Eat ten small fish", said an ancient Jewish sage, "to keep the whole body healthy" (*Avoda Zara* 29a). The fish he had in mind were doubtless the ubiquitous sardine. But of the 18 species of fish in the Sea of Galilee, the most famous is "St. Peter's Fish," which gets its name from the story in Matthew 17:27-18:1.

What kind of fish was this, in whose mouth Peter found a shekel with which to pay the Temple tax for himself and Jesus? We know it was caught by angling - the only reference to angling mentioned in the Gospels. But tilapia, the fish we enjoy now as "St. Peter's Fish", feeds exclusively on plankton and is invariably caught only with nets. The fish caught by Peter and his fishing pole in the Sea of Galilee, say the experts, must have been barbel, a bottom-feeding carp-like predator, hardly a culinary delight in most quarters. Tilapia, however, is a fine-tasting, easily boned fish. In fact, it tastes so good that it became the favorite fish of pilgrims enjoying lunch or dinner on the Sea of Galilee. Thus tilapia was "transformed" over the centuries, to the fish of Matthew's anecdote!

Probably the best-known mosaic ever unearthed in the Holy Land comes from Tabgha, the site of the Multiplication of Loaves and Fishes. A curious fact is that the two fish flanking the loaves in this mosaic do not appear to have come from the Sea of Galilee! They have a double dorsal fin, while all fish known from the Sea of Galilee have only a single dorsal fin. This shows us that the church builders who commissioned this mosaic in the fifth century probably asked an artist from abroad to carry out the work, apparently one who had no inclination to make a study of the actual fish swimming just beyond where he was laying his artistic work.

Fish Dishes

The range of fish dishes, from the most to the least expensive, appears in an interesting discussion between the ancient sages regarding the rules for vows of abstinence. "He is forbidden them, large or small, salted or unsalted, raw or cooked. But he is permitted pickled chopped fish and brine. If he vowed to abstain from small fish, he is forbidden pickled and chopped fish, but he is permitted brine and fish brine."

Fishermen at work on a canal fed by the Nile, in a light boat made of papyrus. The number of fish emphasized their abundance, while showing them in profile demonstrated the diversity of species.

In the non-Jewish world, culinary delights from the sea could include shellfish and fish without scales, forbidden the Israelites according to Leviticus 11:9-12. According to recipes left us by Apicius, a first century CE Roman gourmet, the Romans liked their fish and seafood baked in complex sauces. One recipe for lobster sauce includes "pepper, lovage, caraway, a date, honey, vinegar, wine, fish stock, and mustard." Apicius also suggests serving lobster finely chopped and shaped with eggs, as a stuffing. Poached

Detail of a mosaic depicting fishermen from Um Rassas in Jordan.

Modern-day fishermen on the Sea of Galilee

wings of skate (a flat, diamond-shaped member of the ray family) was another Roman favorite, in a pepper-rosemary sauce, with onion, honey, stock, wine, and olive oil, thickened with flour.

Both the Greeks and the Romans pickled small fish in large vats in their fish-salting plants. The resulting liquid was called *garum* and is mentioned often in Jewish sources. *Garum* could be made from plentiful and inexpensive fish, or rare and costly, such as mackerel, and it appears to have been a staple at all levels of the population. The custom of using fish sauce in cooking was imported to the Holy Land from Syria, Phoenicia, and Greece, and the Talmud makes frequent mention of issues surrounding the adaption of this dish to a kosher cuisine. They used it as relish with fish and eggs, and cooked their meat in it. The famed Rabbi Judah the Prince offers the following riddle-like recipe, "Adda the fisherman told me, 'broil the fish with its brother [salt], plunge it into its father [water] eat it with his son [sauce] and drink after its father [water].'"

The fish market in Acre

Fishing with nets is still a way of life on the Sea of Galilee.

ST PETER'S FISH ON THE GRILL

"When they landed, they saw a fire of burning coals there with fish on it, and some bread."(John 21:9)

The most authentic fish to use in this recipe is Tilapia (fresh-water bass), likely to have been the fish that Jesus prepared for the disciples on the shores of the Sea of Galilee. But any medium-size fish can be substituted.

1/2-1 cleaned, whole fish per person
olive oil
salt & black pepper
sumac
sprig of thyme, hyssop or oregano or 1/2 tsp.
each of dried herbs
grape leaves, if available

Brush the outside of each fish with olive oil.

Sprinkle the fish inside and out with salt, black pepper, and sumaq. Place a sprig of thyme, and a sprig of hyssop or oregano inside the fish. If grape leaves are available, wrap each fish in them before putting it directly on the coals. Cook for about 8 mins. on each side or until done.

Meat: from the Stable to the Table in Bible Days

"All the Choice Pieces" (Ezekiel 24:4)

> *"He who eats meat eats to the Lord"*
> *(Romans 14:16)*

For most of us, planning to have meat for dinner is no more difficult than picking up a neatly wrapped package from the supermarket, checking the label to determine value and freshness, or pointing out our favorite cut behind the glass to our neighborhood butcher. Unlike our biblical ancestors, the involvement of most of us these days in the stages preceding the purchase of meat-raising and slaughtering - is non-existent. But in our appetite for meat at least, human beings have not changed since antiquity.

Some Bible scholars say that meat was only permitted to humanity by default. In the Garden of Eden, where God saw that everything was "very good," God gave Adam and Eve every tree for food, and "every green herb for food" (Gen 1:29-30). Human beings received dominion over other creatures, but did not receive express permission to slaughter them for food. It was only after the flood that humankind was permitted to eat meat (Gen 9:3), commentators say, because God saw that people could not prevent themselves from doing so! Seeing the lack of morality before the Flood, God wanted people to focus what turned out to be their limited moral attention on improving relationships with each other.

In keeping with the idea that meat was not God's first choice for the human diet, the Bible set out numerous rules and regulations to circumscribe its slaughter and consumption. Scripture declares certain animals and birds ritually "fit" or kosher (Lev. 20:25-26). Among the animals, those that split hooves and chewed their cud were considered ritually clean (Lev 11:3-8), as long as they were slaughtered in a manner that was also ritually prescribed - not to cause the animal pain and not to leave behind any traces of blood in the meat (Gen. 9:4, Lev. 7:26-27). It was not permitted to eat an animal that had died of natural causes, or one that had been killed by wild animals (Lev 11:31).

Among the permitted animals, it was forbidden to eat "the tendon attached to the socket of the hip" in commemoration of the story of Jacob's wrestling with the angel who injured him near the tendon (Gen. 32:24-32). Birds of prey were not considered fit to eat. Scholars, seeking a reason for this prohibition, have suggested that the ancients must have felt that "you are what you eat" - that the violent character of these species would enter into those who consumed them.

KOSHER ANIMALS

Ibex

Gazelle

Sheep

Goat

Cow

The sages of the Babylonian Talmud saw in the insertion of the word "from" in the verse regarding commandments for the slaughter "from the sheep, or from the goats" (Ex. 12:15) for families to share at the Passover meal..." an indication that God intended people to be moderate in their consumption of meat. Eating too much meat was considered gluttonous, as Proverbs 23:20-21 notes. Amos criticizes those who "dine on choice lambs and fattened calves" (Amos 6:4) while ignoring the grim realities of the approaching exile. Among the sins that defined a "rebellious son" in the Talmud is one who ate 450 grams of meat!

Limiting the slaughter of animals for food had a practical side to it as well: It would have been difficult to preserve leftover meat, and therefore the family would slaughter an animal only when as many members of the family as possible were present for the meal in order to prevent waste. Another way of preventing waste was to salt meat, in the same way a plentiful catch of fish was salted to preserve it.

Don't Eat What You Can't Afford

In Bible days, pasturing of cattle was a common practice, as Ps. 50:10 lyrically describes: "every animal in the forest is mine, and the cattle on a thousand hills." The wealth of both Abraham (Gen. 12:16) and Job (Job 1:3) is counted in terms of the amount of cattle that they owned.

But much later in the history of the land, during the time of Jesus and in the centuries that followed, the land was increasingly cultivated, leaving little room for pasturing animals. In fact, the rabbis forbade the pasturing of small cattle except in the wilderness areas, because of the harm they do to the environment, especially goats. This made meat all the more rare and expensive at this time.

One teacher, Rabbi Eleazar Ben Azariya, who lived in the period shortly after the time of Jesus, advised that only

people of a certain income should purchase meat every day. Those with a smaller income could purchase a small amount of meat for stew, and those with even less should make do with vegetables or at the most, fish.

Even prosperous people ate meat only at the Sabbath eve meal, and only the very wealthy consumed meat during the week. Others had meat on the table only on the most important holidays. The animals selected for slaughter were usually older ones or calves not suited to the yoke. The costliest meat was calf, because of its greater value in pulling the plow. When we understand this, we can better appreciate the jealousy of the stay-at-home brother in the story of the prodigal son in Luke 15, who complains, "you never gave me even a young goat so I could celebrate with my friends. But when this son of yours who has squandered your property with prostitutes comes home, you kill the fattened calf for him!'" (Luke 15:29-30).

What was on the Meat Menu?

Not burdened with knowledge of the need to limit their cholesterol, the ancients declared their favorite cuts of meat to be the ones with the most fat (although, as with many other health and hygiene issues brought up in the ancient sources, some did warn against the consumption of too much fatty meat). The tail of the sheep was cared for and fostered especially because it could grow large and fat. One source describes a special little wagon that was pulled by the sheep on which their especially large and fatty tail would ride! The breed of sheep common in Israel today still has such a fat tail, weighing some 10-15 pounds. Observers of Bedouin life have noted that even today, a shepherd will tie one back leg of a sheep that tends to stray to this hefty appendage.

In addition to red meat (including wild gazelle that was trapped and brought home to be raised), chicken, pheasant, and peacock were also on ancient menus, with pheasant the most costly of the three. Also on ancient menus were

Cattle grazing on a Galilee hillside.

Baladi Cows at Neot Kedumim Biblical Landscape Reserve

migratory birds in their season, especially quail (Ex. 16:12-13; Num. 11:31-32) which flew in from Europe along their Sinai coast migratory route and were so exhausted after their flight that they could be caught by nets. This is an image that appears often in the Bible, notably, Micah 7:2: "each hunts his brother with a net," and Psalm 140:5, "they have spread out the cords of their net and have set traps for me along the path." Not particularly appetizing to our modern palates were birds' tongues and brains. One element not quite in the category of meat: cooked or roasted grasshoppers and even grasshopper soup! We assume that chickens were kept mainly for egg production rather than their meat, but the question remains open, since the tiny and brittle chicken bones are rarely found in archaeological digs befor the fourth century. Chickens were kept in the courtyards of people's homes; archaeologists believe that special small depressions they have found in the floors of such courtyards were for chicken feed. Jesus uses the mother hen protection of her chicks as a metaphor for the desire to protect Jerusalem (Matt. 23:27)..

Archaeological research has provided interesting evidence of diet and animal husbandry in ancient times. At Shiloh, the Israelite tribal center for over four hundred years animal bones were analyzed from a period of over 2000 years, from the Middle Bronze Age II (about 2000 BCE) to the Roman period. Rib bones from young sheep and goats dominated. In many sites where animal bones were examined, sheep and goats predominate, probably because it was much harder to raise cattle. An exception to this is Tel Nov in the Golan - perhaps the flat pastureland vegetation and numerous water sources in this region made it easier to raise cattle there than elsewhere. In present-day Israel, the Golan is the main area of the country where cattle are raised for meat.

Biblical Bovines - The Baladi Cow

"Baladi" is an Arabic word that means "village." It is also the name of a small species of cow, also known as the "poor man's cow", which has served the farmers of the Land of Israel for thousands of years. Baladi cows are different from modern cows: on average they weigh 180 kg, whereas cows raised by more modern technology are normally around 800 kg. Each cow gives a slim 700 liters of milk per year as opposed to an average of 11,000 liters per cow in the modern dairy industry. Because they weighed little and therefore were not strong, historically the rich had little interest in raising them.

Archaeologists, having found cow bones in excavations, have determined that the Baladi is the direct genetic descendant of the cow of Bible days. Therefore, a closer look at some of their characteristics can help us understand their usefulness to farmers of Bible days as well as to today's traditional farmer. They were more muscular than today's agro-industry cows, which means that they supplied not only milk and meat, but could also be used for plowing. In addition, the Baladi is a hardy breed, surviving almost entirely on wild grasses when no additional food is available, a situation that occurred frequently during the numerous upheavals of Biblical history.

The Baladi cow is almost completely extinct except for a small herd maintained by the Israel Nature and Parks Authority, another one at Neot Kedumim Biblical Landscape Reserve, and perhaps a few kept by traditional Arab farmers.

Mosaic in the ancient Church atop Mount Nebo depicting hunting scenes.

In keeping with Exodus 12:19 and Deut. 16:7, meat that was to be offered in sacrifice was to be roasted. However in 1 Samuel 2:12-14 we are presented with the picture of meat being stewed as in the Ezkiel 'recipe': "Eli's sons were wicked men; they had no regard for the LORD. Now it was the practice of the priests with the people that whenever anyone offered a sacrifice and while the meat was being boiled, the servant of the priest would come with a three-pronged fork in his hand. He would plunge it into the pan or kettle or cauldron or pot, and the priest would take for himself whatever the fork brought up. This is how they treated all the Israelites who came to Shiloh. But even before the fat was burned, the servant of the priest would come and say to the man who was sacrificing, 'Give the priest some meat to roast; he won't accept boiled meat from you, but only raw'. If the man said to him, 'Let the fat be burned up first, and then take whatever you want,' the servant would then answer, 'No, hand it over now.'"

It is possible that at this early period in the history of Israelite practice, while the Israelite cultic center was still at Shiloh, not everyone was following the rules, or that the Hebrew word *bashel* should be used in the English sense of "cook" rather than "boiled" as it appears throughout the Bible, and therefore could indicate that it was roasted meat to which the mendicant priests were helping themselves.

It seems that priestly moderation in the consumption of meat did not improve in Second Temple days. Quite the opposite: The Jerusalem Talmud tractate *Sheqalim* reports that the priests would consume so much meat that it often led to intestinal ailments that a special doctor was kept on hand to treat!

The central meat-eating event in the Jewish calendar was the Passover sacrifice, when the sacrificial lamb would be brought from the home village, or purchased in Jerusalem (for fear that the hardships of travel would injure the animal and make it unfit for sacrifice). In preparation for the meal the animal would be ritually slaughtered, then roasted whole, and eaten by the family together with vegetables and, of course, unleavened bread as in the Last Supper.

Hardly any skulls were discovered, leading researchers to conjecture that the skulls were smashed to remove the brain. Scholars note that in the earlier periods at Shiloh, animals were slaughtered at a young age, indicating their use for meat, while in the later periods they were kept alive longer, presumably to take the best advantage of their renewable resources: milk and hair or wool.

Very few pig bones have been discovered in excavations, with even this small number becoming almost negligible during the Iron Age, when the Israelite tribes are presumed to have entered the Land of Israel. This lack of pig bones has been viewed by some as the first scientific evidence of the incursion of the Israelites, due of course to the dietary prohibition against eating pork.

Cooking the Meat

The parable of Ezekiel (24:3-10) is in purely culinary terms a mouth-watering stew that would suit most of our palates today as well.

The Samaritans celebrate Passover according to the Bible, including the sacrifices.

This round altar dates from the Early Bronze Age (3050-2300 BCE) at Megiddo, and was used by the Canaanite inhabitants of the city to sacrifice animals. Bones of numerous species of animals were discovered in the vicinity of the altar, including one lion bone! This type of altar fits the description of the "high places of the Canaanites," mentioned frequently in the Bible by the prophets, who urged the people of Israel not to participate in pagan sacrificial rites.

Artist's rendering of the altar in the courtyard of the Holy of Holies of the Second Temple in Jerusalem. Priests can be seen tending the fire, bringing the pieces of the sacrificial animal and the wood, and performing various other tasks, while Jews who had brought their animals for sacrifice stand at right to observe the ceremonies.

THE OFFERING OF SACRIFICES

The courtyard, in which stone containers were found, containing large amounts of ash and animal bones.

The altar

A smaller ramp that gave access to a ledge around the altar where priests stood during ceremonies.

The ramp by which the priests brought up the pieces of the slaughtered animal.

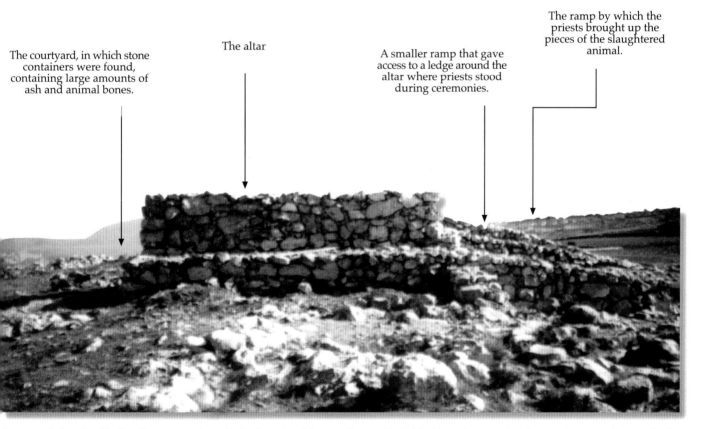

Excavators believe that this altar, discovered on Mount Ebal in Samaria and dating to the second half of the thirteenth century BCE, bears a striking resemblance to the altar of the Second Temple in Jerusalem as described in the Mishna. It may be among the earliest evidence of Israelite worship in the Land of Israel.

Another popular way to cook meat, especially the Passover lamb, was by roasting it on skewers of wood from the pomegranate tree.

Meat for Sacrifice: Difficult to Raise, Difficult to Give Away

Because of the difficulty of raising and caring for the animals, and the accordingly high value of the meat, it is precisely this commodity that was high on the list of sacrifices acceptable to God. Among the many types of offerings for sacrifice, the Bible lists the Sin Offering. Meat sacrificed as a Sin Offering was to be consumed by the priests and to be "eaten in a holy place" (Lev. 6:26). Even the dishes on which they ate attained ceremonial status and were not to be used again, and in fact, were to be broken to ensure this. When the Children of Israel came into the Promised Land and the Tabernacle was set up at Shiloh, the tradition of breaking the dishes was expanded. All of the tribes would gather at Shiloh, bringing their meat for sacrifice. They would sit in family groups on the hills around the Tabernacle, and eat the offering without taking their eyes off the Tabernacle. Then, everyone would break their dishes right there. The discovery of thousands of pottery shards on the hills around the presumed site of the Tabernacle at Shiloh has been reported, confirming this practice.

To Eat or Not to Eat?

Jews as well as early Christians had to deal with life in a society where pagan practice was prevalent. Meat and wine were two of the most prominent foodstuffs offered to idols. In Jewish tradition, kosher slaughtering of animals, and grapes raised by Jews for wine that they produced themselves, solved the problem of coming into contact with possible tainting by idol worship. Among early Christians, the question arose as to whether they, in good conscience, could consume meat that had been purchased in a gentile meat market, and which could have come into contact with pagan ritual. In this matter, Paul counseled, "So then, about eating food sacrificed to idols: We know that an idol is nothing at all in the world and that there is no God but one...But not everyone knows this. Some people are still so accustomed to idols that when they eat such food they think of it as having been sacrificed to an idol, and since their conscience is weak, it is defiled. But food does not bring us near to God; we are no worse if we do not eat, and no better if we do. Be careful, however, that the exercise of your freedom does not become a stumbling block to the weak. For if anyone with a weak conscience sees you who have this knowledge eating in an idol's temple, won't he be emboldened to eat what has been sacrificed to idols?" (1 Cor 8:7-10)

The Quality of Mercy

It is fascinating to note that on the list of animals permitted for food are almost all domestic animals, i.e., animals that have been raised and tended daily, in short, labored over. Animals killed on the hunt would not be permitted because they had not been slaughtered in the prescribed manner. This is no coincidence; scholars see this prohibition as a means of bringing human beings to an understanding of the value of the life they were taking for food.

Lest we think that mercy towards animals is a modern invention, the following Talmudic tale shows its ancient antecedents. "Once, Rabbi Judah the Prince was sitting and discussing Scripture in front of the study house in Sepphoris. A calf running from slaughter ran towards him and said 'Save me!' The rabbi answered, 'what can I do - for this you were created.' For this the rabbi was struck with a toothache for 13 years. And how did his agony end? One day he saw a mouse running in front of his doorway and his daughter wanted to kill it. But the rabbi said, 'let it live.' As it is written, 'He has compassion on all he has made' (Ps. 145:9). And immediately he was cured of his toothache."

In this vein, it should be noted that Deuteronomy 22:67 mandates that mercy be shown to mother birds when collecting eggs, another frequent item on the biblical table. This might even be termed an early "environmental protection" law : "If you come across a bird's nest beside the road, either in a tree or on the ground, and the mother is sitting on the young or on the eggs, do not take the mother with the young. You may take the young, but be sure to let the mother go, so that it may go well with you and you may have a long life" (Deut 22:6-7). Among other benefits, this injunction allows the mother to survive and breed again.

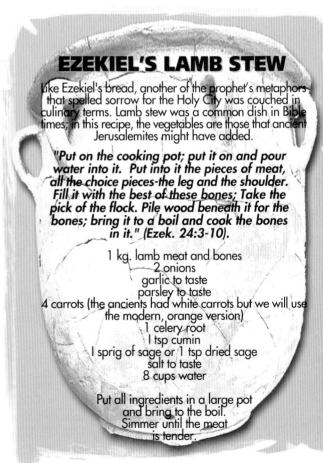

EZEKIEL'S LAMB STEW

Like Ezekiel's bread, another of the prophet's metaphors that spelled sorrow for the Holy City was couched in culinary terms. Lamb stew was a common dish in Bible times; in this recipe, the vegetables are those that ancient Jerusalemites might have added.

"Put on the cooking pot; put it on and pour water into it. Put into it the pieces of meat, all the choice pieces-the leg and the shoulder. Fill it with the best of these bones; Take the pick of the flock. Pile wood beneath it for the bones; bring it to a boil and cook the bones in it." (Ezek. 24:3-10).

1 kg. lamb meat and bones
2 onions
garlic to taste
parsley to taste
4 carrots (the ancients had white carrots but we will use the modern, orange version)
1 celery root
1 tsp cumin
1 sprig of sage or 1 tsp dried sage
salt to taste
8 cups water

Put all ingredients in a large pot and bring to the boil. Simmer until the meat is tender.

Milk and Milk Products

"The Cheese of the Herd" (2 Sam. 17:29)

A traditional sheep pen in the Judean wilderness.

Thousands of years ago, centuries before the first cities were established, the first dairy farmers were nomadic herders. Later, as village life developed, the herding of sheep and goats became one of several agricultural endeavors of village-dwellers as well.

Archaeological surveys of the highlands of Israel and Judah reveal that as people - possibly the first Israelites - began to settle down here in the 12th century BCE, they built courtyard-enclosures next to their homes so they could keep their animals safe at night. A thousand years after the first such enclosures were built, they were still a mainstay of village house architecture. Jesus used such an enclosure as a metaphor: "...I am the gate for the sheep. All who ever came before me were thieves and robbers, but the sheep did not listen to them. I am the gate; whoever enters through me will be saved. He will come in and go out, and find pasture" (John 10:7-10).

The ancient Israelites also kept cows. So did the Egyptians, as Pharaoh's dream of seven fat cows and seven lean cows shows in Genesis 34. But in the Holy Land, such large ruminants could only be pastured successfully in valleys that were wide, flat, and fertile, like the Sharon Plain, the Jezreel Valley, and today's Golan, known in the Bible as "Bashan". Amos, who prophesied to the Israelite northerners, used what must have been a familiar image to hurl an insult at their ladies by calling them "cows of Bashan" (Amos 4:1).

Sheep and goats, on the other hand, had a muscular structure that suited them to grazing the "thin pickings" available in the dry climate of most of the mountainous land of Israel. They could also munch happily on the hardest leaves of the Mediterranean woodlands, even bark, a diet that any self-respecting cow would turn up her nose at. Goats, therefore, and to a lesser extent sheep, were a much more common source of milk than cows.

Dairy farming was a labor-intensive activity; men and women divided the tasks involved. Mesopotamian sculptures from the third millennium BCE show men tending the flocks and milking them, and cylinder seals depict women churning. In the Bible, we find women like Rachel (Gen. 29:7) and Zipporah (Ex. 2:16) tending the flocks closer to home, while the male shepherds, like

A sheep enclosure dating from the Roman era.

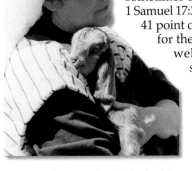

Our scientific advisor, Tova Dickstein, doing some "field research."

Joseph's brothers (Gen. 37:12) and David (1 Sam. 17:15) ventured further afield.

The care of the flock was a constant, sometimes even dangerous task, as 1 Samuel 17:34-36 and Genesis 31:38-41 point out. The shepherd's care for the flocks is a touching as well as a telling biblical symbol, from Ezekiel 34 to Psalm 23, culminating in John 10:2-16, which gave Christianity the memorable image of the "good shepherd". The shepherd is a biblical archetype for a caregiver and a leader.

It is interesting to note, however, that by New Testament times, with cultivation of the land at a high point, shepherds were widely viewed as bad custodians of good land resources, the "thieves and robbers" of Jesus' above-mentioned metaphor. After the destruction of the Temple, the rabbis forbade the raising of "small cattle" for this very reason. Therefore, the impression made on people by Jesus' reference to the "good shepherd" would have been all the greater.

The flock's essential product, milk, also became a symbol in the Bible. In Joel 3:18, it stood for abundance: "And it shall come to pass in that day, that the mountains shall drop down new wine, and the hills shall flow with milk ..." Lamentations 4:7 uses milk as a standard of whiteness, or purity: "Her Nazarites were purer than snow, they were whiter than milk..."

But because sheep and goats are grazed in land unable to be otherwise cultivated, milk in the Bible can have the opposite symbolic meaning as well. In describing the devastation of the Israelite kingdom, Isaiah 7:21-25 uses "milk and honey" not as the biblical symbol of plenty that we are used to, but quite the opposite: "In that day, a man will keep alive a young cow and two goats. And because of the abundance of the milk they give, he will have curds to eat. All who remain in the land will eat curds and honey. In that day, in every place where there were a thousand vines worth a thousand silver shekels, there will be only briers and thorns...As for all the hills once cultivated by the hoe, you will no longer go there for fear of the briers and thorns; they will become places where cattle are turned loose and where sheep run."

The First Cheese

An ancient legend relates that the discovery of cheese was made by a young shepherd boy in about 4000 BCE, when he found that some milk that had pooled in the bottom of his leather sack had fermented. The thirsty boy could not help himself; he drank it, and found to his surprise that it was delicious! Fermented milk products did originate in

To this day, flocks are herded at Shepherds' Field on the outskirts of Bethlehem

the Fertile Crescent, and may have indeed been an accidental discovery made by nomadic shepherds. Cheese, of course, would coagulate on its own quickly enough in the hot Near Eastern climate, absorbing microbes from the air that turn the milk sugar into acid. But the first churning would have been a natural outcome of the swinging back and forth during travel of the convenient storage pouches travelers had made for their milk from the stomachs of sheep, camels, or goats. The process was sped up by the presence of an enzyme in the animal stomach, rennin (known commercially as rennet), that fostered the production of acid-producing bacteria in the milk.

As religious observance developed, the sages of the Talmud were naturally concerned that milk should derive from a ritually clean animal as mandated by Scripture. But in the case of cheese there were other issues too: the Mishnah expresses concern that the cheese, if it were manufactured by gentiles, might have been curdled in the stomach of an unclean animal, one not properly slaughtered, or one sacrificed in idol worship.

To avoid the ritual problems regarding the animal origin of rennet, the ancients discovered an alternative in the sap of certain trees, such as the fig or a mysterious extinct plant called balsam. In one source, we find them discussing whether, if the sap derived from a tree under three years old (whose fruit was prohibited by the Bible) it could be used as rennet. Modern experiments have recreated cheese in the ancient way, using the milky excretions from every part of the fig tree, including the leaves, to curdle milk.

Goat's milk was a staple of nomadic life.

Since meat was eaten sparingly in ancient times, animals were normally raised for their dairy products. As 1 Corinthians 9:7 points out, "Who plants a vineyard and does not eat of its grapes? Who tends a flock and does not drink of the milk?" Proverbs 27:26-27 notes that careful care of the flock will produce profits: "the lambs will provide you with clothing, and the goats with the price of a field. You will have plenty of goats' milk to feed you and your family and to nourish your servant girls." Goats were reared principally for their milk, which was preferred to that of any other animal. (Modern nutrition experts agree that goat's milk and cheese are more easily digested than other kinds of milk or cheese.) Especially among nomadic peoples, milk and its byproducts would have been one of their most nourishing available foods. It is no wonder that Yael, wife of Heber the Kenite, whom we can deduce was a nomad because she invited Sisera into her tent, stored her milk in a skin (a container often used by nomads because of its ease of transport) and served milk to the tired and ill-fated Canaanite general (Judg. 4:18-21).

But What Does "Milk" Mean?

Not all biblical translations agree on the meaning of the Hebrew words for the various milk products mentioned in Scripture. In its simplest form, the Hebrew word *halav* could simply mean milk as we know it. But in the hot climate of the Holy Land, this liquid would not have remained fresh for long. When the New Testament refers to milk as a food considered suitable for infants until they could digest other foods, it is likely to have been a reference to mother's milk (1 Cor. 3:2, Heb. 5:12, 1 Pet. 2:2).

The recipe for salty goat cheese, known as "Feta" in Greek, is centuries old.

In most cases biblical "butter" is not the same as our butter; it more likely indicated soft curds containing varying degrees of fat. For example, medieval Jewish scholar Rashi suggests that "butter of kine" (Deu. 32:14) should be understood as what we would call cream today. Cheese, as mentioned in 1 Samuel 17:18, 2 Samuel 17:29 and Job 10:10 may have been a milk product pressed into a form and dried in the sun. This kind of cheese is called *'afiq* by the Bedouin and is still produced today in much the same way - it can be kept for long periods and re-hydrated when ready. *'Afiq* can be seen for sale in the markets of the Old City of Jerusalem and of Acre. This long-standing feature of the local food supply shows us that in ancient times,

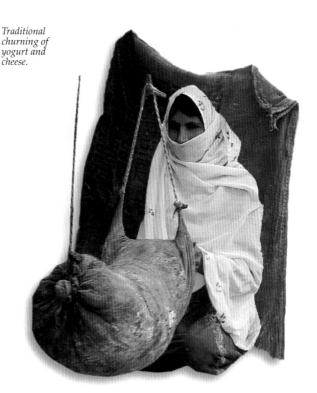

Traditional churning of yogurt and cheese.

the city depended for its supply of milk products on the village-flock and the nomadic herdsmen.

The manufacture of milk products begins with the process of churning, in order to separate the fatty materials from the liquid. In this part of the world, traditional churning is carried out by rocking the liquid back and forth inside of a sack made of goatskin suspended from a wooden stand. The churning takes about an hour and a half, more if the weather is cold. When churning their milk in winter, the Bedouin of today add hot water to the sack and light a fire nearby in order to speed up the process. The cheese water is siphoned off and salt is added to make the *'afiq*, the dehydrated cheese.

Siphoned off - but not discarded. When we modern cooks open a package of cheese and discover it floating in water, we carefully pour the water down the kitchen drain. Not so in the ancient kitchen! The cheese water, known in the sources as *qom*, was preserved as a refreshing drink in and of itself.

This flock of sheep patiently seeks out edible greens in their rocky "dining room."

The Akeldama (Matt. 27:8) Monastery is located on the approach to the "Cheesemakers' Valley" or Tyropoeon in Jerusalem, probably the city's cheese market in Jesus' day.

Dairy Delicacies

Jewish dietary laws, mandating the absolute separation of milk products and meat products, have been the origin of an imaginative array of milk-based recipes which make for a varied menu at meals that are "dairy". The present-day holiday table of *Shavu'ot* (Pentecost) is a good place to find mouth-watering dairy dishes. But over the centuries a great deal has changed in this regard. In the Bible, *Shavu'ot* was originally the celebration of the grain harvest, and animal sacrifices (later consumed by both the priests and the people) were a hallmark of the holiday. In later history, as the sages linked Pentecost to the giving of the Ten Commandments, meat disappeared from the holiday menu, replaced by a host of dairy dishes. This tasty tradition originated with the idea, based on Genesis 1:29, that in the Garden of Eden Adam ate only vegetables and fruit. It expresses the desire, on the day that commemorates the giving of God's perfect rules, the Ten Commandments, to go back to that "more perfect world". Another origin of this tradition may be found in Song of Songs 4:11 where the sages voiced the hope that the Bible would be as satisfying to people as "milk and honey...under your tongue."

The fatty substances then coagulate into a very thick sour cream. The Bedouin cook the cream in a cauldron over the fire together with sage and *hawaij*, a savory seasoning. The resulting product can be kept for several weeks. There is still a third, even richer cream that is produced during the churning. This product, which the Bedouin call *zabda*, has the appearance of modern butter, deep yellow in color. But unlike butter, it can be kept for many years. It is used in cooking in the same manner as olive oil. Lamb and rice are also cooked in this thick cream in a festive dish called *mansaf*.

In ancient Mesopotamia, cheese making was an important task. Archaeologists there have found cylindrical seals depicting a shepherd and his flock, and rows of little circles which were probably meant to represent cheese. In the days of the Greeks, a kind of porridge made of barley-meal, honey, wine, and grated goats' cheese is mentioned in the writings of Homer. By Roman times, the option of smoking cheese had been discovered. At the time of Jesus, cheese seems to have been a popular food: an entire valley in Jerusalem was identified by Josephus as Tyropoeon, the Valley of the Cheese Makers. Ancient sources from this period mention the existence of a special implement, a "grater for cheese" that was probably not that much different from our modern ones.

Pottery cheese strainers dating from the Neolithic and the Bronze Age show the antiquity of cheese making. Special containers were discovered during the excavation of tombs from the Plain of Sharon from the Middle Bronze era (around the Age of the Patriarchs). These large jars were discovered with a small plate within. The plate had a hole in the center, likely for suspension by a rope from the top of the container, to be filled with whatever substance served them as rennet, lowered into the container, and later withdrawn. The finding of these containers in tombs demonstrates that the loved ones of these ancients wanted to make sure they had the equipment they needed in the next world to produce what was obviously considered an indispensable food.

THE MATRIARCH SARAH'S CHEESE FOR CHILDREN

"He then brought some curds and milk and the calf that had been prepared, and set these before them." (Gen. 18:8)

Sarah might have just finished making a batch of this simple cheese when the angels showed up at her tent-flap. This is a fun and easy recipe to make with young children.

2 pints milk
A few drops of fig sap - today we use a few drops of lemon juice for the same result.
(The branch of a fig tree is what the biblical matriarch probably used to stir!)
salt
1 tbsp. butter
1/2 tsp. dried hyssop

Heat the milk. Add the fig sap or lemon juice and stir with the fig branch or wooden spoon. Bring slowly to a boil. When curds have separated from the liquid, take a clean cloth with a wide weave ("cheesecloth") and pour the contents of the pot into the cloth. Wring out the cloth to get rid of as much liquid as possible, leaving the cheese curds behind. Place the cheese in another container. Add salt, butter, and hyssop to taste.

$\mathcal{B}$iblical Sweets

"What is sweeter than honey" (Judges 14:18)

Scientists tell us that virtually from birth, babies have a natural preference for sweets. It is therefore not surprising to find that sweet foods have played a part in the human diet as far back in history as the evidence can stretch. And as human culture advanced, culinary ingenuity added more and more sweets to diets.

Sugarcane, our major modern-day source of sugar, does not appear in the Bible (notwithstanding the "fragrant cane" of Jeremiah 6:20, which was a perfume plant and not sugarcane). Sugarcane probably came to the Holy Land around the first century BCE, when Roman historian Strabo reports that "a reed in India brings forth honey without the help of bees, from which an intoxicating drink is made though the plant bears no fruit." Interestingly, in its earliest form, sugar cane was used as a medicine and not as a sweetener.

The first evidence of honey production comes from the Caucasus Mountains and northern Turkey, where the openings in tree trunks where wild hives were located were widened by human labor to allow for easier access to the honey. Taking a leaf from the book of nature, as time

Gustav Dure's famous rendering of Samson wrestling a lion. In its carcass he later finds a beehive, the basis for a riddle he posed to the Philistines (Judges 14:5-14).

went on, people began to use logs they themselves had hollowed out to house bees. Of course, logs normally do not survive through time to provide historical evidence, but Carbon-14 testing on two such lone logs that did survive showed one to date from the first century BCE, and the other from the third millennium BCE Bronze Age.

The first evidence of truly domesticated bees comes from an Egyptian bas-relief dating from 2400 BCE. In a clay vessel manufactured around 1900 BCE, a hunk of beeswax and the leg of a bee were discovered. The ancient Greeks created artificial hives as early as the eighth century BCE.

Since domesticated honey did not appear in the Bible lands until the Hellenistic period, biblical honey was aptly described as "honey from the rocks" (Deut. 32:31) - honey that flowed accidentally into rock crevices or bushes, or where Jonathan found it "on the ground". In the Bible, Samson ate honey when he found a beehive in the carcass of a lion (Judg. 14:8-9). He later used this incident to tease his friends with a riddle: "Out of the eater, something to eat; out of the strong, something sweet" (Judg. 14:14). When Jonathan ate the honey he found, he broke an oath his father Saul had made that the entire army should fast until the battle against the Philistines had been won. But Jonathan excused his behavior by describing the quick jolt of energy,

A beekeeper depicted on the wall of the 6th-century BCE tomb of Pasaba, a royal Egyptian steward.

A honeycomb from a tree trunk.

the "brightening his eyes", which he implied the entire army could have used to win the battle (I Sam. 14:25 ff). In the New Testament, John the Baptist (Matt. 3:4) ate honey as he moved through the wilderness preaching. The New Testament book of the Revelation also uses honey in the same context as the Hebrew Scriptures - as the ultimate sweet: "I took the little scroll from the angel's hand and I tasted it, and it was as sweet as honey in my mouth..." (Rev. 10:9), a verse that echoes Psalm 119:103, "How sweet are your words to my taste, sweeter than honey to my mouth."

The Power to Kill and to Heal

We will never know who owned the unfortunate sweet tooth that first proved that the honey that bees manufacture from some flowers, such as rhododendron and oleander, can be poisonous. Those consuming this honey suffer from severe dizziness, muscle weakness, which can last a few hours, and may even die. In the early fifth century BCE, thousands of soldiers led by the Greek warrior Xenophon fell ill from consuming poisoned honey. The soldiers of Pompey, Roman conqueror of the Holy Land, found mysterious honey cakes placed along a road they traveled near the Black Sea. Unfortunately for them, they fell into temptation, and gobbled them up greedily. They never reached the battlefield.

But honey is also one of humankind's earliest medicines. An Egyptian papyrus contains a list of 900 remedies for various illnesses. Over half of them contain honey. It was considered particularly useful in the treatment of eye diseases, burns, and other wounds. Ancient Egyptian women even used it as a breath freshener, chewing a mixture of herbs and incense shaped with honey into balls.

As the book of Proverbs 25:16 puts it, honey is to be "sweet to the soul, and health to the bones". What the ancients knew instinctively has been proven under the microscope

in our age: mineral- and amino acid-rich honey contains an enzyme known as glucose oxidase, which increases the amount of peroxide in the body and destroys harmful microorganisms. The Talmud recommends honey mixed with wine as a treatment for diarrhea, a use to which homeopaths put it today as well. Royal jelly, produced in glands in the jaws of young bees, also contains a high amount of broad-spectrum antibiotic. Honey has been rediscovered as an aide in healing infections and against poor appetite.

Propolis, a material culled from plants and mixed with wax and pollen, which the honeybees use to seal their hives, has the strongest antibiotic properties of any element of honey and was used to preserve fruit.

Mysterious Manna

Exodus 16:31 said that manna "tasted like wafers made with honey." Of what was the sweet substance made that was so satisfying to the ancient Israelites as they wandered in the wilderness? One theory holds that manna is secreted by a species of insects that feed on the tamarisk tree, which grows commonly in arid zones. The insects secrete excess carbohydrates (would that we all could do that!) in a liquid form that dehydrates rapidly in the dry desert air to become particles that resemble "thin flakes, like frost on the ground" (Ex. 16:14). Scientists have determined that this substance contains three kinds of sugar plus pectin.

A Bee or not a Bee

"A land flowing with milk and honey": this verse appears 40 times in the Bible and is perhaps the best known verse used to describe the Holy Land. However the meaning of the word "honey" is not so simple: most ancient commentators knew of several different fruits that, when pressed or processed, could produce a product as sweet as bees' honey. They therefore saw "milk and honey" as describing a land in which there is much cattle to produce milk, and marvelous fruit trees.

The "honey" of Deuteronomy 8:8, is likely to have been date honey.

One notable exception to assigning "honey" to fruit trees is Isaiah 7:22. When we look at the verses surrounding the phrase in question, we understand that this prophet of

In nature, bees create their hives in a tree

In nature, bees create their hives in a rock

Judah's destruction at the hands of Babylon had turned the famous image strikingly around - using it as one of destruction rather than as a blessing. "In that day, a man will keep alive a young cow and two goats. And because of the abundance of the milk they give, he will have curds to eat. All who remain in the land will eat curds and honey...As for all the hills once cultivated by the hoe, you will no longer go there for fear of the briers and thorns; they will become places where cattle are turned loose and where sheep run" (Isa. 7:22-25). Cattle and bees, we can deduce, can only live in open spaces and in forests where agriculture is not practiced.

Beehive in a tree trunk

Subtitle: Eating With Honey

Honeycombs were eaten raw, but by Roman times a honey wafer was served, as well as other kinds of cakes, each of which was known by a different name. Jam was made with roasted linseed or poppy seed and served with honey, and certain wildflowers were served dipped in honey. Candies made of honey, called *dulcia*, were also prepared. Honey was also an important component in both meat and vegetable sauces. Mead was a drink prepared in Roman times by fermenting honey. The very wealthy enjoyed a kind of sherbet created by mixing honey and snow, and fruit juices enriched with honey were served. As in our times, dessert was served at the end of the meal; at more formal meals, which the Greeks called *symposia*, this course was accompanied by wine. It is likely that natural sweets served as the simplest kind of desserts; in wealthier homes, a special pastry chef was retained.

ASHISHOT

"Strengthen me with raisins, refresh me with apples" (Song of Songs 2:5)

In this recipe you will find neither raisins or apples! The meaning of the Hebrew word for the second of the "love tonics" (Song of Songs 2:5), *ashishot*, is unclear. English Bible translations render it either "apples" or "flagons"." The opinion of one ancient rabbi has given us the following, nearly 2000-year-old recipe for a confection, whose name we have left in its original Hebrew.

8ozs red lentils	3-4 tblsp. honey
1 tblsp. whole wheat flour	1/2 tsp cinnamon
3-4 tblsp. honey	1/4 cup olive oil

Toast the lentils well in a frying pan. Grind them very fine into flour (Use a coffee grinder if available). Mix the lentil flour with the olive oil, making dough balls the size of ping-pong balls. Flatten the balls into small pancakes. Heat additional olive oil in a frying pan and fry the pancakes gently on both sides until golden brown.

A colorful collection of spices in the Jerusalem market.

Herbs and Spices

"All the finest spices" (Song of Solomon 4:14)

though they were not mentioned in Scripture because ancient commentaries show us that they were common during New Testament times, and we can therefore imagine them on the table wherever Jesus dined.

Aloes (Num. 24:6 Ps. 45:8, Prov. 7:17, Song of Solomon 4:14, John 19:39).

Experts say that the aloes of the Bible derive from the sap of the eaglewood tree (*Aquilaria agallocha*) native to India. Aloes retain their fragrance for many years, a characteristic that would make them useful for anointing the dead (John 19:39), because of the Jewish custom of entering the cave-tomb often for ceremonies or subsequent burials of additional family members. The American aloe, or agave, is a succulent, and not to be confused with the biblical aloes.

Anise (Fennel) (Matt. 23:23)

In Talmudic times the seeds of this dill-related plant, which grows wild in Israel, were sprinkled on bread before it was baked.

Anise plants and seeds. The wild plants perfume the air of Israel's mountains with a licorice aroma in the fall.

Bay tree (Laurel)

Nehemia (8:15) probably meant to include the bay tree as the second item in its list of trees from which booths are to be constructed for the Feast of Tabernacles. But the name "bay tree" is absent. This is one of the many cases in which the various English translations of the Bible do not agree. The literal translation of the Hebrew is to be found in the New King James version of the text as "oil tree". This name, too, is ambiguous, but scholars identify it as the bay tree because by the second century CE, oil was indeed the trademark product of the bay tree. It was one of the many spices used, not to flavor food as today, but as an ingredient in perfumes.

Bay leaves.

> "And she gave the king... large quantities of spices, and precious stones. Never again were so many spices brought in as those the Queen of Sheba gave to King Solomon." (1 Kings 10:10)

The herbs and spices considered indispensable in the modern kitchen make our food taste better, more exotic and, with the advent of greater nutritional awareness, we know that they have the potential to make us healthier. Our biblical ancestors, however, did not always connect herbs and spices to food; sometimes they were entirely unrelated to it. Non-food uses for spices were extensive: spices were used as perfumes (Est. 2:12, Song of Songs 4:10, 5:1; 13:6, et. al.), and were an indication of wealth (2 Kings. 20:13). Because of their pleasing aroma, they were also seen as an acceptable and desirable part of worship, essential to the creation of the incense burned in the Tabernacle and later the Temple (Ex. 25:6, 30:22-38, 1 Chron. 9:29-30).

With regard to the ancient kitchen, one food-related use of some herbs and spices that is lost to us in these days of refrigeration: the not-always-welcome aromas of meat and other perishables could be disguised by the use of certain spices while others, such as pepper and salt, acted as preservatives.

Many fertile areas of the Holy Land had become neglected due to abandonment over the centuries, a process that began to be reversed only in modern times. A "desert" land was often immortalized in drawings and photographs created by travelers and consequently, many people even today continue to wrongly perceive the country as a wilderness that produces little in the way of plants. In fact, quite the opposite is true. The dry mountain climate of the Holy Land actually is very conducive to the flourishing of many aromatic plants. The heat of a midsummer's day is the perfect time for plants like marjoram and sage to release their perfume into the air.

Below is a list of some of the most famous Biblical spices and herbs. As noted, some plants produced fragrances and were not used in food, but they appear here because the Bible classes them as spices. Other spices appear even

Cinnamon (S. of S. 4:14, Prov. 7:17, Rev. 18:13)

Cinnamon comes from the bark of a species of cinnamon tree apparently native to China. The cinnamon tree eventually migrated to the Holy Land (S. of S. 4:14) where it flourished until the destruction of the Temple. An ancient commentary on the Book of Genesis says that cinnamon-log fires burning in Jerusalem bestowed a fragrant aroma on the whole city. Known more for its fragrance than its flavor in antiquity, it was one of the ingredients in the incense used in the Tabernacle (Ex. 30:22-32), and Proverbs 7:17 portrays a woman of doubtful repute using it among the spices perfuming her bed.

Cinnamon sticks.

Black Cumin (Isaiah 28:27)

An annual that produces black, sesame shaped seeds which are sprinkled on bread and cheeses. Isaiah - where the name of the spice is sometimes mistranslated as "dill" or ordinary cumin - says that when harvested, it was threshed with sticks to release the seeds from the seed pod. The mother of a certain rabbi, says a talmudic source,

A blossoming black cumin plant.

used to bake bread with black cumin, and then scrape it off. We cannot be sure of the reason for this, but it could be that some regarded this spice as a healthy food additive, while others feared it as nearly poisonous.

Cumin (Matt. 23:23)

At the time of Jesus, cumin, native to Israel, grew profusely in the wild and was even exported. Ancient physicians believed it to be effective in stemming the flow of blood. Mentioned together with mint and dill on Matthew's list of spices that were tithed, cumin was a popular seasoning for meat.

Coriander

An annual herb of the carrot family originating in the Mediterranean region and, like many other spices, was introduced by the Romans to Europe. Coriander seeds, exotically aromatic as they are, come from a plant whose leaves give off such an unpleasant smell that the Greeks gave it the name *korus*, after a species of bug! The Roman naturalist Pliny tells us that the best coriander came from Egypt, so we may imagine that the Israelites brought this plant with them to Canaan.

Coriander bears a resemblance to parsley - but the taste and aroma of coriander are unforgettably more exotic!

Fragrant Cane (Calamus) (Ex. 30:23; Jer. 6:20)

Sometimes mistaken for sugar cane, this plant, identified by some botanists as ginger grass, was used as a perfume and as embalming oil. Explorers who opened tombs of the pharaohs in 1881 noted that the sweet aroma of ginger grass wafted out.

Gall (Wormwood) (Ps. 69:21, Lam. 3:15, Matt. 27:34 et al.)

The power of gall as a biblical metaphor for bitterness is well earned, as it is one of the bitterest-tasting herbs known. The Romans did give victors in athletic races wormwood to drink because it was thought to be healthy. Indeed, for centuries wormwood was considered an important element of the botanical pharmacy, helpful in relieving stomach pains.

Stalks of gall (wormwood).

Hyssop (Num. 19:6, Lev. 14:4, Lev. 14:49, John 19:29 et al.)

Hyssop was an ingredient used in the preparation of the ashes of the Red Heifer (Num. 19:6) and in the water used for the purification of lepers (Lev. 14:4). On the fateful Passover of the Exodus, a branch of hyssop was used to

Hyssop plants in bloom.

brush the blood of the Pascal Lamb onto the doorposts of Israelite homes (Lev. 14:49). The modern-day Samaritans, who carry out the laws of the Pentateuch exactly as written, still use hyssop in their Passover rites. In John's account of the Crucifixion (John 19:29), Jesus was given a vinegar-soaked sponge on a hyssop branch. I Kings 4:33 may reveal the symbolism of hyssop's use in these contexts: there, lowly hyssop, which "grows out of the wall" is contrasted with the lofty cedar tree, and therefore it became a symbol of humility. However the words from Psalms "cleanse me with hyssop" (Ps. 51:7) may be more than symbolic - research carried out at the Hebrew University of Jerusalem has shown that hyssop does have infection-fighting properties.

Hyssop, together with some other members of the marjoram family, are native to the Holy Land and surrounding countries. Thyme, salt, and toasted sesame seeds, combined with hyssop, produce the locally popular spice mix *za'atar*, which is sprinkled on bread or mixed in sauces in modern-day Israel.

Mint (Matt:23:23)

Mint was valued for its aromatic oil and as a seasoning for meat.

Mustard (Matt. 13:31, 17:20, Mark 4:13, Luke 13:19, 17:6)

The mustard plant (Sinapis alba), nourished by winter rains, grows rapidly and by spring its white or yellow flowers brighten fields and roadsides across the Holy Land. By the end of summer its pungent seeds are ready for harvest. The seeds of this species, and its other relatives in the Cruciferae family from which the condiment is derived, are tiny (about (1 -3 mm or 1/8 of an inch across) making it the perfect symbol of faith as Jesus used it. The mustard plant also grows both rapidly and large in relation to the size of the seed. However, because this mustard plant does not normally grow to the size of a tree (Matt. 13:31, Mark 4:31, and Luke 13:19), scholars once believed that another shrub, *Salvadora Persica*, was meant in the famous parable.

Myrrh (Gen. 37:25, Ex. 30:23, Ps. 45:8, Es. 2:12, S. of S. 1:13, Matt. 2:11; John 19:39, Rev. 18:13, *inter alia*.)

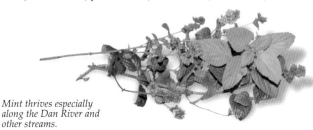
Mint thrives especially along the Dan River and other streams.

Among the first Christmas gifts (Matt. 2:11), myrrh gained its greatest fame in the ancient world, together with frankincense (Isa. 60:6; Ex. 30:34) as a fragrance rather than a spice for food (Ps. 45:8, S. of S. 1:13, *inter alia*.). However myrrh was used as a spice to make inexpensive wine more palatable. It was common to offer this mixture to condemned criminals in Roman times, and indeed was offered to Jesus on the Cross (Mark 15:23). Myrrh derives from a tree native to Arabia, Ethiopia, and Somalia. Whereas frankincense, that other famous First Christmas present of the Three Wise Men, comes from trees that are incised to produce the sap, the best myrrh comes from the sap that oozes naturally from the tree. When the sap hardens, it is ground and added to ointments and creams. New Testament scholars have noted that myrrh was not only among the first gifts offered to Jesus, it was also the last: As John 19:39 records, it was one of the spices with which the body of Jesus was anointed for burial.

Nard (Spikenard) (S. of S. 4:13, 4:14, Mark 14:3, John 12:3)

This plant has its botanical origins in the Himalayan Mountains. A member of the valerian family, nard was highly valued not only because of the perfume that was produced from its roots, but also as a sedative. The word nard comes directly from the Hebrew name of the plant. Its full name comes from the many spikes that emanate from the root.

Rue (Fitch) (Luke 11:42)

Rue, a Holy Land plant that made its way to Europe.

A shrub native to Mediterranean regions. The Romans brought rue from this area to England where, much later, Catholic priests used bunches of the plant to sprinkle holy water on participants in religious ceremonies. Thus the plant found its way into Shakespeare's Richard II as the "herb of grace". This type of shrub grows wild, but can also be cultivated. The garden variety was tithed, which earned it a place on Luke's list of items tithed by the errant Pharisees.

Saffron (S. of S. 4:14)

Saffron is produced from the flowers of a very ancient member of the crocus family with Mediterranean origins. Song of Songs 4:14 is our proof that ancient biblical farmers cultivated it as far back as First Temple times (1000-586 BCE). In mishnaic times, the plant was raised in order to harvest its yellow stigmas (the part of the pistil of the flower that receives the pollen grains) that were dried and used in perfumes, cooking, medicine, and as a dye. The high cost of the spice (in ancient times, worth its weight in gold!), was due to the fact that only three stigmas can be collected from each flower. Then, as now, "counterfeit" saffron was often marketed to unsuspecting customers.

Sage

Though not mentioned in the Bible, sage nevertheless figures prominently in Holy Land lore. One legend relates that when Joseph and Mary were escaping the wrath of Herod to Egypt with the baby Jesus (Matt. 2:13-14) and the Roman soldiers were perilously close, a sage plant (which normally reaches about 3 feet in height) miraculously grew high enough to shelter them. The Arabic name for the plant, *maramiyah*, comes from the local

Sage plants are most at home in the rocky Holy Land hills.

pronunciation of Mary's name. It hints at another popular legend, that Mary used the leaves of the sage to ease her labor pains. Sage tea is an important component in traditional and alternative medicine for the relief of cramps, among other ailments.

Sumaq

Some members of the Rhus family, of which sumaq is one, are poisonous and the cause of an itchy rash to which many a careless venturer into a North American forest can attest. But the berries of *Rhus coriaria*, the sumaq common in the Holy Land, are a sought-after food additive to this day. They are ground into a reddish-brown powder and added to meat and other dishes to impart a tangy astringent flavor. Sumaq served the same purpose in ancient times as lemon (unavailable in the ancient Holy Land) does for modern diners.

A sumaq plant.

Salt

Salt is first mentioned in the Bible in a directive that it be added to all the offerings in the Tabernacle (Lev. 2:13). Salt was a preservative of meat and, on a practical level, it could have served as such in the Tabernacle in the wilderness. But its use points up an important spiritual lesson: because of salt's preservative properties, the "covenant of salt" mentioned in Numbers 18:19 and 2 Chronicles 13:5 symbolized permanence. The words of Ezra 4:14, "under obligation to the palace", literally translated from the original Hebrew, become "eating of the salt of the palace" - meaning strong, everlasting loyalty.

A lump of pure salt congealed from the water of the Dead Sea.

"The world can live without wine, but not without water. The world can live without pepper, but not without salt." - ancient Jewish saying.

People who have bathed in the Dead Sea (the source of salt in Bible days) and have seen their small cuts and scrapes disappear almost miraculously, have experienced the cleansing and disinfectant properties of salt in the most direct way. Elisha's throwing of salt into the waters of Jericho to purify it (2 Kgs. 2:20-21), and rubbing newborn infants with salt (Ezek. 16:14) can be understood in this context.

Salt was so essential to people in Roman times that wages were paid in salt, giving us the modern word "salary" in addition to various sayings such as being "worth one's salt."

A preservative and health-inducing a condiment as it may be, and in minute amounts a fertilizer (Matt. 5:13, Luke 14:34), salt also had the connotation of infertility and destruction (Deut. 29:23, Job 39:6, Jer. 17:6, Zeph. 2:9). When Lot's wife disobeyed God, she was turned famously into a pillar of salt (Gen 19:26). In Judges 9:45 we read that when Abimelech captured Shechem, he sowed it with salt, so that nothing would grow there. The same sense can be gleaned from Jeremiah 48:9, "put salt on Moab, for she will be laid waste."

Jesus used this most common of condiments as a symbol: "You are the salt of the earth. But if the salt loses its saltiness, how can it be made salty again? It is no longer good for anything, except to be thrown out and trampled by men" (Matt. 5:13). It was easy for people to understand this,

These particular pillars of salt on the Dead Sea shore bear no resemblance to the unfortunate Mrs. Lot.

because they saw salt was placed on the table in a lump on a small dish, together with the soil that got mixed in with it during the mining on the shores of the Dead Sea. When all of the white crystals had been picked out of the dish and sprinkled over the food, the remaining soil, with tiny bits of salt that were worthless as flavoring, was indeed "tossed out to be trodden underfoot" (Matt. 5:13).

HERBAL BIBLICAL BREAD

"Taking the five loaves and the two fish and looking up to heaven, he gave thanks and broke the loaves." (Mark 6:41)

We recommend using a wok for this bread-and-spice recipe - but not in the usual way! We have taken "culinary license" with the bread mentioned in this verse, relying on the frequent references to bread seasoned with spices in sources contemporary with the time of Jesus.

1 kg. whole wheat flour
water as needed to create the dough
1 tsp olive oil
1 tblsp hyssop.

Mix all ingredients. Make dough balls the size of ping-pong balls then flatten them. Rub the outside of the wok with olive oil and turn it upside-down over a gas flame. Place the flattened dough over the center of the wok to bake, turning it over once.

Keeping Food And Keeping it Fresh in Bible Days

"The Stock and Store and the Whole Supply of Bread" (Isa. 3:1)

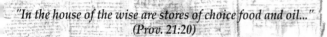

"In the house of the wise are stores of choice food and oil..." (Prov. 21:20)

A loaded caravan sets out across the desert in the detail of this drawing by David Roberts, 1839.

It had been a good year. The soft earth had yielded easily to the plow; the seeds had taken root and sprouted effortlessly. Rain had come in its season, and the harvest was plentiful.

But there remained still one more problem that could make or break not only the individual farmer, but a whole village, and even, as the Bible teaches in the story of Joseph's long-term planning for Egypt, a whole country. There were drought years and ensuing famines to face, wars, and pestilence. Any or all of these threats could wipe out the food supply. And therefore the problem was how to store the food, protect it, have it available for distribution, and preserve its freshness.

The Bible tells us in great detail how Joseph's interpretation of Pharaoh's dream of "seven fat years and seven lean years" resulted in the construction of storehouses that saved Egypt: "The seven years of abundance in Egypt came to an end, and the seven years of famine began, just as Joseph had said. There was famine in all the other lands, but in the whole land of Egypt there was food. When all Egypt began to feel the famine, the people cried to Pharaoh for food. Then Pharaoh told all the Egyptians, 'Go to Joseph and do what he tells you.' When the famine had spread over the whole country, Joseph opened the storehouses and sold grain to the Egyptians, for the famine was severe throughout Egypt. And all the countries came to Egypt to buy grain from Joseph..." (Gen. 41: 53-57).

The earliest peoples sought solutions for the existential challenge of food storage even before they built permanent houses in which to live: they dug small storage pits, carefully lining them with stones. Such pits have been discovered in the Jordan Valley, dug into the floors of the circular dwellings that pre-date by thousands of years even the famous "first city in the world" at Jericho. Stone-lined storage pits (that still contained large quantities of burnt grain) were discovered in the remains of the early Canaanite city of Arad (2900-2700 BCE). Similar pits were dug into the ground at Dan, Hazor and Lachish; they are considered a means of dating the entrance by the still-nomadic Israelites into the Promised Land.

The storage pit at Megiddo, site of the Biblical Armageddon, with its capacity of some 12,800 bushels, dates to the period of the Israelite kings. Its huge dimensions show that it was a communal pit, and must

The grain silo at Megiddo from the time of King Jeroboam of Israel.

A storage pit at Tel Dan that may have been created by the first settlers of the Tribe of Dan.

have stored grain that came from surrounding villages, transferred as taxes to the king or to be kept in case of attack on the hinterland that would have brought a large number of refugees into the city.

Archaeologists note that the granary at Megiddo appears not to have had a cover, which would have rendered it rather inefficient. This was not because granaries with covers did not exist elsewhere. A model of such a grain storage system was discovered in a tomb in Upper Egypt dating to the third millennium BCE, much earlier than the Megiddo granary. The Egyptian system consisted of 12 round silos that lined three sides of a square courtyard, effectively sealed with pointed covers.

In recent excavations at Motza, near Jerusalem, 36 granaries were discovered. Dug into the ground and lined with stone, some of the deepest were two meters deep and 1.5 meters wide. It can be deduced from this that Motza was an important center supplying Jerusalem and the vicinity with grain.

The design and quarrying of the pit, the collection of the grain, and its movement to the city were all tasks requiring a great deal of organization. Workers of all

The recently discovered First Temple-era granaries at Motza

kinds had to be hired (or slaves imported), housed, and paid. Contracts had to be made to hire pack animals and wagons, and guards employed to ensure the safe arrival and protection of the grain. This work would have required a complicated system of symbols to record the numerous transactions involved; some historians believe that the fact that the earliest of these communal storage pits appear around the same time as the first written symbols is not a coincidence, but that the primary human need for writing had its root in this very purpose.

Grain was among the products stored in large jars like this one, known as pithoi.

Archaeologists studying the effectiveness of these storage pits have noted that as much as 40% of the produce may have been destroyed by mildew or eaten by rodents. For us modern folk, with every conceivable means at our disposal for containing and preserving food, from our kitchen cabinets and our pantries, to our deep freezes, fridges, dry ice and Styrofoam, this would be an unacceptable loss. But for the ancients - who at the time of Jesus noted that a person storing food with his neighbor may incur losses depending on the amount and the passage of time - the remaining edible grain could have made the difference between starvation and survival.

Large-scale storage of food was essential at one site in the Holy Land that was almost as big as a small city: the Temple. Nehemiah 13:5 explains why, noting that the Temple contained "...a large room" in which to store "the grain offerings and incense and temple articles, and also the tithes of grain, new wine and oil prescribed for the Levites, singers and gatekeepers", as well as the contributions for the priests.

These jars held olive oil in a second-century CE cave storage facility at Amazia in Israel's lowlands. They were placed in small hollows carved in the floor, connected to each other by channels. If a jar broke, the oil would flow from the hollows through the channels to a point where it could be collected again.

A collection of storage jars and other vessels from Jerash, Jordan (Roman period)

Malachi 3:10 also mentions a special storehouse in the sacred precinct.

At Home with Food Storage

Though storage pits and granaries continued in use throughout ancient times, beginning in the Chalcolithic period (4300-3300 BCE), the pottery jar was a great advancement in the storage of foodstuffs. It could be easily covered and transported, and created in a variety of shapes and sizes for every conceivable use.

The collared-rim storage jar, most associated with the settlement of the Land of Israel by the Israelite tribes, was apparently used for the storage of liquids, olive oil, wine, and water. Large-size jars, with a capacity of anywhere from 250-1800 liters and known to the archaeologists as *pithoi*, were also used to store grain as early as the Chalcolithic period (4300-3300 BCE). Other foods that had been dried for later consumption were also stored in jars of various sizes. Giant size storage jars, containing as much as 1800 liters, have also been discovered. Larger storage jars are a sign of a settled population, because nomads need a size and shape of jar that is convenient to carry on the shoulders or on a beast of burden. For example, the "jug" (1 Sam. 26:11, 1 Kings 17:14, *inter alia*) had flat sides and was designed to be attached to a belt worn around the waist like a modern-day canteen (water bottle).

The storage jar also became a means of not only containing and preserving foodstuffs, but also of

protecting them from theft, as smaller ones could be kept in one's house. Matthew 5:15 attests to this practice: "...neither does one light a lamp and place it under a bushel." A "bushel", probably the Hebrew *eifah*, was a measure of grain weighing some 22 liters.

Grain was only one of the commodities stored in pottery jars. Various types of dried vegetables and fruit were also kept in people's homes. Another testimony to the custom of keeping foodstuffs within the house during this period is noted in the Babylonian Talmud: "...a man says to his agent, 'bring [a small measure] of wheat to my upper chamber...but if you have not mixed it with some sandy soil containing salt [to preserve it from vermin] it is better not to bring it up.'"

The storage of perishable liquids was also considered. By around 2900 BCE, archaeologists tell us, the custom of keeping milk in specially crafted containers for later consumption was well advanced. In Bible days, milk was sometimes kept in skins (Judg. 4:19). In the Talmud, the sages suggested that milk kept in jars in the home should be covered for fear that a poisonous snake could creep into them. One ancient source used food storage as a metaphor: "just as water, wine, and milk can become unfit through inattention (i.e., by not returning the cover after use) so can the words of Scripture be forgotten through inattention." The average wine storage jar could hold some 350 liters.

Water was kept in large jars in the courtyards of people's houses, filled by smaller containers that could be carried or placed on the back of a beast of burden. Water for ritual washing was kept in large stone jars, because it was believed that stone was impervious to ritual impurity (John 2:6). Large jars were also used to store wine. These were lined within with tar to ensure imperviousness, and sealed with a cork made of straw and mud. Jars were also used to store sauces, vinegar, oil, and honey. Some of these jars were apparently large enough to contain a human being - at least according to the story about fourth-century BCE Greek philosopher of self-sufficiency, Diogenes of Sinope, who took up residence in a large storage jar or barrel.

Lids reveal that these jars held perishable liquids or other commodities.

Stove and silos found in the tower of the western wall of Masada, which was probably used as a bakery during the revolt of 73 C.E. ▷

An Egyptian potter brings alive Jeremiah's image of the potter in Jeremiah 18:3-6.

As far back as the fourth millennium, potters began using wheels to produce their goods. Decorations on pottery were very rich right from the beginning of the technology, and varied in technique and design from region to region. As cities developed and trade flourished, pottery was imported from one place to another, and a certain kind of pottery from "abroad" found in a dig can reveal volumes about trade relations and culture. For example, at Megiddo in the Jezreel Valley, teapot-shaped vessels from Syria were discovered, dating from the third millennium BCE, with hallmark white horizontal or wavy lines. At excavations at Tel Anafa in the Hula Valley of northern Israel, were enough fragments of a wide, shallow pan from the Roman era to deduce that it was used to make *patinae*, a kind of Roman-style quiche.

Food Storage in Jesus' Day

A parable of Jesus, recorded by Luke, illustrates how life should not be lived, using food storage as a backdrop. "The ground of a certain rich man produced a good crop. He thought to himself, 'what shall I do? I have no

Caves like this one beneath the Basilica of the Annunciation in Nazareth may have served as storage facilities beneath the home.

place to store my crops?' Then he said, 'this is what I will do. I will tear down my barns and build bigger ones and there I will store all my grain and my goods. And I will say to myself, you have plenty of good things laid up for many years. Take life easy; eat, drink, and be merry.' But God said to him, 'You fool! This very night your life will be demanded from you. Then who will get what you have prepared for yourself.' This is how it will be with anyone who stores up things for himself but is not rich toward God" (Luke 12:16-21).

A look at the huge storehouses that Herod the Great ordered constructed near his personal residence at Masada are the perfect example of the point Jesus was trying to make. Josephus Flavius, in his book The Wars of the Jews, notes that the rebels who took the fortress of Masada at the beginning of the Great Revolt in 66 CE found the storehouses still full of food, preserved by the dry air at this desert site above the Dead Sea. He quotes the speech of the rebel leader Eleazar Ben Yair who, when suggesting that the people of Masada take their own lives when about to be defeated by the Romans, demands that they leave the Roman invaders "nothing except our provisions; for they will be a testimony to us when we are dead that we are not subdued for want of necessaries."

Herod's storehouses at Masada.

Ancient sources relate that at the time of Jesus, each major city would collect a certain amount of food in a central facility. A second-century commentary on the story of Joseph in Genesis 41:48-49 relates that, "Joseph collected all the food produced in those seven years of abundance in Egypt and stored it in the cities. In each city he put the food grown in the fields surrounding it", in terms of the cities with which his pupils and colleagues were familiar: "He gave that which was in Tiberias to Tiberias, that which was in Sepphoris to Sepphoris, since every land gave its own produce."

Josephus Flavius also mentions such storehouses in Jerusalem in the Wars of the Jews, when describing the infighting among the Jews themselves during the war against the Romans. He reports that the head of one of the rival parties, John of Gischala, "set on fire those houses that were full of corn, and all other provisions."

Keeping Things Fresh

A second-century commentary on the story of Joseph as viceroy to the Pharaoh speculates on the means by which Joseph kept the grain he had collected in good condition, revealing a method of food preservation popular in the days when the commentary was written: "Joseph had ashes and earth mixed with salt strewn on the garnered food from the very soil on which it was grown. Also, he preserved the grain in the ear, all these being precautions to guard against rot and mildew."

"Solomon's Stables" at Megiddo may have had areas that served as storage facilities for caravans stopping off at this crossroads city.

Like most food related issues, the preservation of food interested the ancient rabbinic sages for the most part insofar as it related to Sabbath observance. For example, only certain materials were permitted as insulation materials to keep food warm over the Sabbath, when a fire could not be lit. Among these materials were the wings of a dove, sawdust, and soft material that remained after the manufacture of linen cloth. Food was also kept warm in baskets lined with wool. Other materials, like *gefet* (the crushed material left behind after the pressing of olives, also used as a fuel), salt, sand, or... manure, were forbidden as insulating materials. The reason? They were simply too effective! So believed medieval sage Maimonides in interpreting the ruling, noting that these materials continue to cook the food, an act that is forbidden on the Sabbath. Simple burial in the ground was considered a permissible as well as effective way of keeping the hot things hot.

Burial in the ground was also a way of keeping cold things cold during the long hot months in the land of Israel. Sometimes, vessels would be immersed in water for this purpose. In the Jerusalem Talmud, keeping water itself cool, as well as wine, was accomplished - among the wealthy - by storing them in snow! This custom persisted into later periods as well, with the snow reaching Egypt from Syria by swift horse, an

Drying grapes in the sun to be stored and consumed at a later date.

expensive proposition doubtless available only to the upper classes.

Other methods of preserving food included pickling (especially of vegetables like olives and onions and fish), salting (olives and fish), and smoking (mainly of meat). Pickling of vegetables was carried out using a number of special vessels, by a method many present-day home-picklers would recognize: sealing the vegetables in a vessel with water, salt, and vinegar.

Another way of preserving food was to boil water together with spices and place within it the food to be preserved. Foods like watermelon, squash, cabbage, and chard, could be conserved for several days using this method.

Silos in the grotto under the Church of St. Joseph in Nazareth

The Last Supper - The Most Famous Meal in History

"Dip(ping) Bread into the Bowl" (Mark 14:20)

"The Teacher asks: Where is my guest room, where I may eat the Passover with my disciples?" (Mark 14:14-15)

The Last Supper was the backdrop for some of the most significant exchanges between Jesus and the Disciples. It is a unique part of history and heritage that Jews and Christians share, because that meal which Jesus shared with the Disciples was a Passover meal, known as the Seder, still an important part of Jewish observance today. Let's take a closer look at the elements of the meal.

Preparations

Matthew 26:19 reports that "the disciples did as Jesus had directed them and prepared the Passover." Would that we could open that succinct sentence like a picture book! According to John 19:14 the day was "the day of preparation for the Passover Week." There would be a distinctive hustle-bustle throughout Jerusalem, entire families working hard at the many tasks involved in the preparation of the meal.

By Jesus' time the custom was deeply rooted of seeking out even the slightest crumb of leavening, in order to more graphically remember that the Children of Israel were in such a hurry to leave Egypt that they did not take time to let the bread rise (Ex. 12:39). In fact, all food products containing or suspected of containing leavening would be buried until the Passover week had concluded. Crumbs were found in nooks and crannies with the help of the extra light of an oil lamp - there is even a modern Hebrew saying that comes from this practice: to look for something very carefully is "to seek with a lamp." (Nowadays the ceremony is done with a wax candle.)

The table is set for the recreation of the Last Supper at the Ein Karem Biblical Resources Institute.

A family at the Passover table: From the 18th century Van Geldern Hagaddah

This day, one day before Passover, already had a holiday feeling about it, not only because of the excited preparations at home, but also because the people had begun to arrive from miles around to Jerusalem, bringing their Passover sacrifice to the Temple. In the Galilee, it was said that the only people who worked on this day were those whose services were needed because of the impending holiday, such as tailors, shoemakers, barbers, and launderers, and...caterers. Ancient sources say that it was common practice to have a large meal catered, but if any of the food was spoiled, the caterer was liable for a fine!

According to a medieval source, Rabbi Akiva, a sage who was known for his studiousness, sent the men of his study house home early on the day of the Seder itself, so they could put their children to bed for a nap to have them wide awake for the Seder. Need one ask where mother was during this time? Busy with the preparations, of course.

The Menu

As it is today, the Seder meal was one of the most significant family events in the Jewish calendar. The hallmark of the meal is its specific order, which is the meaning of the Hebrew word *seder*. The Seder begins with the blessing over the wine, with a total of four cups of wine to be imbibed during the meal. According to one interpretation, the four cups of wine correspond to the four expressions of deliverance employed in Exodus 6:6-7: "I will bring you out...deliver you...redeem you, take you to me." During the meal, the story of the Exodus from Egypt was related, and eventually read from a book called the Hagaddah, with the active participation of all present, especially children. This custom comes from the Hellenistic tradition of holding a festive meal of which a symposium was part and parcel. Children's curiosity was already piqued by the fact that they had been given sweets before the meal, in order to prompt them to ask "Why is this night different from all other nights?" This is one of the "Four Questions" asked by children during the course of the

ceremony preceding the meal. After drinking the first cup of wine, a course of vegetables would be served.

Interestingly, though the Pascal Lamb was an indispensable element of the meal, it was not the main course. We know that Passover diners were required to eat a piece of the Pascal Lamb only the size of an olive, and so we understand that its presence on the table was symbolic and not culinary. The lamb, a yearling, was offered in thanksgiving because God passed over the houses of the Israelites during the plague of the first-born in Egypt. Therefore, other dishes would obviously be served at the Passover table, including other kinds of meat. We cannot know exactly what was in the bowl into which Jesus dipped together with his betrayer (Matt. 26:23; Mark 14:20). It could have been stew made from another kind of meat, lentil stew, or vegetables.

As is still the custom today, as the Seder commenced, the head of the family took the unleavened bread in his hands and proclaimed, in the same Aramaic language that was spoken by Jesus, "This is the bread of affliction. Let all who are hungry come and eat." It is not difficult to imagine Jesus using these very words when the Gospels report that, "Jesus took the bread, gave thanks, and broke it."

In its earliest days, preparation of the paschal animal was a domestic ceremony, from the slaughter to the roasting (as it still is among the Samaritans, who perform the rituals exactly as described in the Bible, in Deuteronomy 16:7 and Exodus 12:8-9). After the reforms of King Josiah, the celebration of Passover was transferred to the Temple of Jerusalem, and with it the custom of slaughtering the paschal animal and having the meal in the courtyard of the Temple. But eventually, people would bring their animal to

A Yemenite Jewish family at their Passover table - on a mat on the floor, just as their Biblical forefathers ate.

"Elijah's Cup" is set in the center of every Passover table, symbolizing the desire for the coming of the Messiah.

be sacrificed at the Temple, and then roast it outside the Temple precinct. The animal would be roasted on skewers made of pomegranate wood, in small convex clay outdoor ovens. The ovens would be manufactured each year especially for Passover, springing up in courtyards all over Jerusalem, like "mushrooms after the rain." Speaking of which, concern about the "latter rains" ruining the new ovens was serious, with one sage warning people to bring their Passover ovens into the house when a rainstorm was pending.

Since the sacrificing of the animals would continue until sundown in keeping with the description in 2 Chronicles

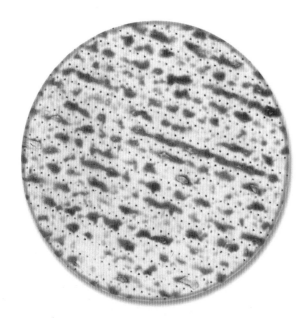

Modern-day matzah, unleavened bread.

35:13, we can imagine that, cooking time considered, people would not sit down to eat before nine o'clock in the evening. A very important custom was that no less than ten people sit together at the Passover meal,

symbolizing the unity of the people before God in worship. If a family group happened to be smaller than ten (a rare occurrence), two families combined their resources (and their paschal lamb) and celebrated together.

A bitter herb, in remembrance of the bitterness of slavery, was on the table. Among the bitter herbs that were used were mallows, chicory, and radishes. The bitter herb was dipped in a mixture known as *Haroset*. In the possible Hebrew origin of this word, *heres* which means clay, is its symbolic importance, because it was meant to remind the diners and have the appearance of the mortar that the Israelite slaves used in constructing the store-cities of Pithom and Ramses. To know how the ancient people made their *Haroset*, we look to the traditional Jewish communities which use the fruits that grew in the Land of Israel in Bible times: grapes, wheat (matzah meal), dates, figs, olives, apricots, pomegranates, and almonds - are used. Modern North African Jews often include pine nuts and hardboiled eggs, and sometimes add strong spices like ginger.

Eryngo one of the plants used for the bitter herbs of the Passover meal.

Like many customs associated with Temple worship, with the Temple's destruction, the offering of the paschal lamb came to an end. However, the custom is recalled in present day Seder meals by the Seder plate, a platter placed in the center of the table and containing the various symbolic elements of the meal, which include a lamb shank.

At the end of the meal, the group of Psalms known as the Hallel (Psalms 113-118) are still sung, as reflected in Matthew 26:30 and Mark 14:26.

RECLINING AT THE LAST SUPPER

This picture, created by the Biblical Resources Institute in Ein Karem, suggests a possible seating (or rather, reclining) arrangement at the Last Supper, around the three-sided table known as the *triclinium*. The left wing of the table was the most important, with the host occupying the second position from the end. To the left and right of the host were positions of honor (Matt. 20:21,23), with the left position considered the most important. Having arranged the meal and taught during its course, we may assume that Jesus sat in the host's position. According to custom, one normally rested on one's left elbow and ate with the right hand. Therefore John, who was leaning on Jesus' chest (John 13:3), must have been to the right of Jesus.

Who was given the seat of honor on Jesus' left? Was it Peter who, Luke 22:8 reports, was in charge of preparations? The evidence may indicate otherwise: First, when Jesus announced that one of the disciples would betray him, Peter had to motion for John's attention to get him to ask Jesus who the betrayer would be (John 13:23-26). But the person on Jesus' left at the table faces away from the others. To get John's attention, Peter had to have been reclining at the opposite (right) wing of the table. We can be even more specific: The account of Jesus' washing the disciples' feet hints that Peter was the last to have his feet washed (John 13:6), meaning that he was down at the far end of the right wing of the table. Perhaps after Jesus offered the seat of honor to someone else, the impulsive Peter angrily took the furthest place at the opposite corner!

There are two indications that it was Judas who occupied the seat of honor next to Jesus. Bread dipped in the dish was customarily offered to the guest of honor; John 13:26 reports that Jesus offered it to Judas. And Judas had to have been reclining near Jesus to have been able to dip his hand in the same bowl (Matt. 26:23). Apparently Jesus, although aware of Judas' planned perfidy, extended him every courtesy and opportunity to relent. If this reconstruction is correct, says Dr. James Fleming, director of Biblical Resources, Jesus' leaning on Judas' chest during the meal must have heightened the conflict in Judas' heart (Matt. 26:14-16).

"In Remembrance of Me"

Biblical Weights and their Equivalent in our Terms

Have you ever known a fine cook who, when asked for a recipe, seems unable to accurately describe the measure of some ingredients that make their dishes delicious? Being told to add "half an eggshell" of this or that may be frustrating to some. Yet the Bible is familiar with this system: its smaller units of measure were based on the human body: One unit was a *kometz*, the "handful"; Lev. 2:2; 5:12 - the amount that three fingers of a hand can grasp. The "hollow" of Isaiah 40:12 is the entire palm of the hand, also mentioned in Ex. 9:8, as "handfuls." People also measured using the size of containers they had at home, the volume of which is far from clear to researchers (I Sam. 1:24). Ancient cooks may have prepared some of their dishes using fixed-size portions of ingredients, whose volume has also been lost to us. This is the reason why in some verses, the Bible speaks of quantities in numbers of portions without designating the volume (I Sam. 25:18; II Sam. 16:1, et al.). Nevertheless, from certain internal equations given by the Bible, such as Exodus 16:36 and Ezekiel 45:11, Ezekiel 45:14, we are able to calculate the weight and volume of some of the measurements used in Scripture.

Commonly mentioned units of volume mentioned in the Bible are:

Ephah (Ex. 16:36; Ezek. 45:11, 13; 46:14, et al.): usually rendered "bushel" in the King James version of Mark 4:21: a dry measure equal to approximately 5.80 gallons (22 liters).
Homer (Lev. 27:16; Isa. 5:10; Ezek. 45:11; 13:14; Hos. 3:2): approximately 58 gallons (220 liters) and equal to a kor (Ezek. 45:10).
Kor (Hos. 3:2) (10 ephahs): A weight equal to a homer.
Letekh (5 ephahs): approximately 29 gallons (109 liters).
Bath (Ezek. 45:11, 14; II Chron. 2:9): A liquid measure equal to an ephah.

Se'ah (Gen. 18:6; I Sam. 25:18; I Kings 18:32; II Kings 7:1, 18; et al.): approximately 2 gallons (7.6 liters).
Hin (Ex. 29:40; Ezek. 45:24; 46:11, 14, et al.): approximately 1 gallon (4.2 liters).
Omer (1/10 of an ephah) (Ex. 16:16, 36; Lev. 23:10-14, et al.): 6 gallons (approximately 25 liters).
Kab (II Kings 6:25): approximately 1.3 quarts (1.2 liters).
Log is the small liquid measure, (Lev. 14:10 et. al.): approximately 0.63 pints (31 grams).
Gerah (1/20 of a shekel according to Exodus 30:13; Lev. 27:25; and may be one of the "seed pods" of 1 Kings 6:25) about 0.6 grams.

Cylindrical cups of this type, ranging in height between 5 and 15 centimeters, are frequently found in sites of the Second Temple period. It is believed that their capacities correspond to the dry and liquid measures mentioned in the Mishnah.
These vessels were pared with a knife or adze, and their surface was left unsmoothed. The vertical handles rule out the possibility that they might have been produced on a rotating lathe.

A table for measuring liquids. Limestone, Maresha, Hellenistic period, 143 BCE.

Biblical Recipes

*T*he Bible contains no true recipes as we understand the term - a set of instructions for making food. The closest it comes might be the mixture of grains that God commanded Ezekiel to bake into bread (Ezek 4:9), the purpose of which was of course allegorical rather than nutritional.

The ancient Greeks did set down some of their recipes in writing, a practice that was expanded by the Romans during the time of Jesus. However they gave no quantities, and sometimes, because of language or cultural differences, we do not know what some of the ingredients were. The ancient Jewish commentary on the Bible, the Mishna, contains descriptions of dishes that approach recipe status, but they needed only to allude to the elements or processes involved because they were entirely familiar to them, and we are therefore left with many intriguing questions. Some of these are answered when we look at the dining customs and foods of the Bedouin, aspects of whose lifestyle still reflect ancient practices. Most of our recipes, in which we have made sure to use only ingredients available at the time (and also today), are based on authentic Greek, Roman, and Mishnaic dishes.

Many of the recipes were provided by Neot Kedumim Biblical Landscape Reserve, where attempts are made to re-enact various aspects of life at the time of the Bible.

All recipes serve four.

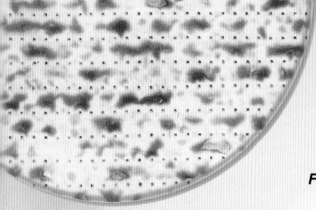

For delicious, authentic Biblical bread, bake under coals.

Israelite Unleavened Bread

"They baked cakes of unleavened bread"
(Exodus 12:39)

The Israelites leaving Egypt did not have time to let their bread rise.

• 2 cups whole-wheat flour
  (if possible durum wheat)
• ¾ cup cold water
• 2 tbsps olive oil
• 1 tsp salt
Can add any Biblical flavoring: hyssop, onion, garlic, sesame seed, sumac etc.

Combine the flour, olive oil and salt with the water to form a dough and knead for 3 minutes. Add chosen flavorings. Divide into 8 balls. Flatten each into a thin round and prick with a fork. Cook individually on an inverted wok over a hot cooking stove, or bake on a greased cookie sheet for 10 minutes in a hot oven (500°F, 250°C).

Sarah's Biblical Bread

"Get...fine flour and knead it and bake some bread" (Gen. 18:6)

In Bible times, packaged yeast did not exist, so people used sourdough starter which absorbed yeast from the air.

Starter:
• ¾ cup whole-wheat flour
• ¾ cup warm water
Mix flour with water in a glass or ceramic bowl and leave uncovered in a warm place for four days, stirring occasionally.
Dough:
• 6 cups whole-wheat flour   • 2 cups hot water
• 2 tsps salt   • 2 tbsps olive oil

Place the flour, water and salt in a bowl and add the starter mixture. Mix to form a dough. Knead on a floured surface with floured hands for at least 10 minutes. Place in a bowl and brush all over with olive oil. Cover and leave to rise for 3-4 hours. Preheat the oven to 350°F (180°C). Knead again and shape into two small loaves. Place on a baking sheet and bake for 1 hour.

❖ ❖ ❖ ❖ ❖ ❖ ❖

Tabernacle Bread-Cakes (Pita)

The ancients did not know the properties of yeast but discovered that fruit peel, especially of grapes and apples, fermented the dough.

• ½ - ¾ cup fresh grape juice
• 5 cups whole wheat flour
• 1/4 tsp salt   • 1 tsp olive oil

"Cakes of bread made without yeast and mixed with oil." (Lev. 7:12)

Make grape juice by grating seedless grapes into a cup, with the peel.
Mix the flour, salt and oil. Slowly add the grape juice, mixing well, until a flexible dough is formed. Knead. Leave for two hours and knead again. Divide into fist-sized balls. Flatten and roll each into the shape of a pita bread. Place on an inverted wok or pan over a cooking stove. Cook on both sides until golden-brown.

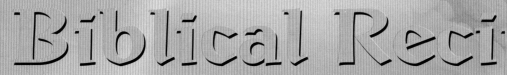

Columella's Salad or Dip

Columella lived in Spain and Italy in the first century C.E. Most of his writings were about viticulture, but he also recorded some recipes.

- 3-6 lettuce leaves,   • ½ cup chopped parsley
- ½ cup chopped mint leaves
- ¼ cup chopped rocket
- 2 tsps chopped rue or rosemary (optional)
- 2 tbsps hyssop leaves (optional)
- ¾ cup feta cheese, crumbled
- 1 tsp salt   • 1 tsp freshly ground pepper
- ¼ cup olive oil   • 2 tbsp wine vinegar
- ½ cup chopped walnuts (optional)
- 1 tbsp toasted sesame seeds

Tear lettuce leaves into bite-size pieces and place in a bowl. Add the remaining ingredients and toss lightly. Pound in a mortar or blend in a food processor for a smooth dip.

❖❖ ❖❖❖❖❖❖ ❖

Cheese Dip

"Curdle me like cheese" (Job 10:10)

- 6 ozs feta cheese
- 2 cups thick Greek-style yogurt
- 2 tbsps chopped dill   • 2 tbsps chopped parsley
- 2 tbsps chopped mint
- ½ cup chopped walnuts (optional)

Mash the feta cheese with a fork and mix well with the yogurt. For a stronger taste add less yogurt. Add the herbs.
Serve with Biblical Bread, pieces of carrot, celery, cucumbers.

Jael's Labaneh

Made by the Bedouin to this day

"She brought him curdled milk"
(Judges 5:25)

- 4 cups sheep's milk
  (if not available, regular milk will do)
- 2 tsps yogurt   • 1 tsp salt
- 1 tbsp olive oil
- chopped dill, hyssop, mint (optional)
- minced garlic (optional)
- 1 cucumber, quartered lengthways and sliced
  (optional)

Gently heat the milk, bring to the boil and simmer for 1 minute. Remove from the heat and cool slightly. Mix 3 tbsps of the milk with the yogurt and add to the remaining milk. Put in a glass bowl, cover tightly, and leave for at least 8 hours in a warm place. Add the salt and pour the mixture into a large strainer lined with a cheesecloth. Tie up the cloth and suspend it over a basin for 10-12 hours. Put in a glass container and cover with olive oil. Add chopped fresh herbs, garlic, and season to taste. Can also add cucumbers. Serve with Biblical Bread.

❖❖ ❖❖❖❖❖❖ ❖

Cato's Cheese Bread

"All who remain in the land will eat curds and honey" (Is. 7:22)

- 2 cups feta cheese, well-drained
- 1 cup flour   • 2 eggs
- 12 bay leaves   • 4 tbsp honey

Put the cheese in a bowl and mash until smooth. Add the flour and beaten eggs to form a sticky dough. Divide into four quarters and form round, flat loaves from each. Place loaves on greased baking sheets with three bay leaves under each. Bake in preheated oven at 400°F (205°C) for 1-1½ hours. Remove from oven and spread with honey.

Biblical Recipes

Jesse's Vine Leaves Stuffed with Cheese

"Take along these ten cheeses"
(1 Sam. 17:18)

- 20 vine leaves, fresh or preserved
- ½ cup olive oil
- ¼ cup wine vinegar

Filling:
- 10 ozs medium-soft goat cheese
- 2 tbsps thick yogurt
- 2 tbsps sesame seeds

If using fresh leaves, simmer in boiling water for 10 minutes to soften. Preserved leaves should be rinsed well. Combine the olive oil and vinegar, bring to a boil and pour over vine leaves. Marinate for two hours or longer. Drain.

Combine the filling ingredients, mixing till smooth. Separate the vine leaves and place 1-2 tsps of filling in the center of each leaf, depending on size. Fold over the stem end, then fold in the sides and roll up tightly. Place in a serving dish, join side down.

❖ ❖ ❖ ❖ ❖ ❖

Honeyed Yogurt

"a land flowing with milk and honey"
(Ex. 3:8)

Per person:
- 8 ozs Greek-style yogurt
- 3 tsps honey
- 1 oz shelled unsalted pistachio nuts

Place yoghurt in a dish, whisk until smooth and stir in the honey, leaving a marbled effect. Sprinkle with pistachio nuts.
Can also use as a dip for fresh fruits.

Shobi's Globi

"honey and curds...cheese from cows' milk"
(2 Sam. 17:29)

- 1 cup semolina
- oil for frying
- 1 cup ricotta cheese
- honey

Mix the semolina flour and ricotta cheese to make a thick dough. With wet hands, form medium-sized balls. Fry in oil, turning frequently, until golden-brown on all sides. Drain on kitchen paper, roll in honey and serve. Can be sprinkled with sesame seeds or poppy seeds.

❖ ❖ ❖ ❖ ❖ ❖

Roman Wafers

"a little honey, some spices and ... almonds"
(Gen. 43:11)

- ½ cup grape juice
- ½ cup chopped almonds or nuts
- 1 cup flour
- ½ tsp cinnamon
- ½ tsp chopped rosemary
- 4 tbsps honey
- 2 eggs
- ¾ cup milk
- olive oil for frying
- honey for garnish
- ½ tsp freshly-ground black pepper

Heat the grape juice and boil to reduce to 1/3 cup. Mix all ingredients except for the pepper, place in a double-boiler or a pot inside a pan filled with water, and cook until thick. Spread mixture in a flat pan and when cool, cut into squares. Heat oil in a pan and fry the squares until golden. Dip the squares in warmed honey and sprinkle with black pepper.

Biblical Recipes

Vegetables & Pulses

In Old Testament times, people ate stews into which they could dip bread rather than soups. In Roman times, however, soups were popular.

Pharaoh's Molokhia Soup

"Every green plant for food" (Gen. 1:30)

This recipe is based on an ancient text found in Pharaonic tomb paintings.

• 4 cups chicken stock
• 1 lb molokhia leaves or Swiss chard, finely chopped
• 2 tbsps olive oil
• 3 finely chopped garlic cloves
• 1 tbsp ground coriander
• salt & freshly-ground black pepper • 1 tsp flour

Heat the chicken stock, add the molokhia or Swiss chard and bring to a boil. Simmer for 15 minutes. Meanwhile, fry the garlic in olive oil until golden and stir in the coriander. Add to the soup together with the seasonings and mix well. Mix flour with a little water and add to the soup, stirring until well-blended. Bring to a boil and season to taste. Serve hot.

Jacob's Lentil Soup

"Then Jacob gave Esau some bread and some lentil stew" (Gen.25:34)

• 1½ cups split red lentils
• 6 cups chicken or vegetable stock
• 1 medium onion, cubed • 2 sticks chopped celery
• 1 leek, chopped • 1 carrot, cubed
• ½ tsp ground cumin • 1 tbsp white wine vinegar
• salt & freshly-ground black pepper
• 1 medium onion, sliced • olive oil

Put the lentils in a pot with the stock and vegetables and bring to a boil. Simmer for 30 minutes, until the lentils have disintegrated. If too thick, add water. Add cumin and wine vinegar and season to taste. Fry the sliced onion in the olive oil until almost caramelized and add to the soup. Serve hot with croutons.

Lentil and Barley Stew

"Ahab said to Naboth, 'Let me have your vineyard to use for a vegetable garden'" (1 Kings 21:2)

• 3 tbsps olive oil • 1 cup chopped onions
• 1 chopped garlic clove • ½ cup diced carrots
• ½ cup diced celery • 4 cups vegetable stock
• 1 cup lentils • ½ cup barley
• 1 tsp cumin • ½ -1 tsp salt
• ¼ tsp black pepper • 1 bay leaf

Sauté the onions, garlic, carrots and celery in the olive oil until soft. Add the remaining ingredients. Cover, bring to a boil and simmer over a low heat for 45 minutes, until the lentils and barley are tender. Discard the bay leaf and season to taste.

Biblical Recipes

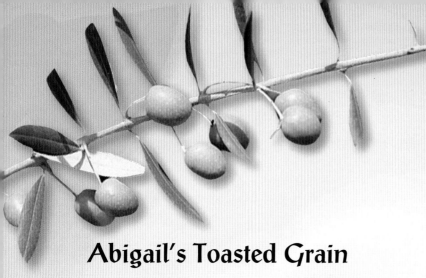

Abigail's Toasted Grain

"Abigail lost no time. She took... about a bushel of roasted grain..." (Josh. 5:11)

This was the easiest and quickest way to eat wheat, and also preserved it longer. It was especially popular for taking on journeys.

- 1 lb whole wheat kernels
- 1 tsp salt
- water
- 1 tsp olive oil (optional)

Heat a wok or frying pan and pour in the seeds and salt. Stir constantly until lightly browned. Sprinkle a little water over while toasting, to soften the seeds. Eat as you would popcorn.

Gideon's Barley Cakes

"A round loaf of barley bread came tumbling into the Midianite camp" (Judges 7:13)

- 1½ cups barley flour
- ½ cup wheat flour
- 1 cup milk
- 1 egg
  - 1 cup liquid honey
  - pinch of salt

Sift the flours and salt. Mix in the milk and egg, stirring constantly, and add the honey. Preheat the oven to 220°C (425°F). Drop spoonfuls of the mixture on a greased baking tray, leaving space for the cakes to spread. Bake 10-15 minutes, until done.

Flavored Olive Oil

"I give you all the finest olive oil" (Numbers 18:12)

You can make olive oil more "biblical" by adding herbs available in Bible days.

Per 8 fluid oz (or medium sized) bottle, one sprig of your choice of:
- Rosemary or
- Hyssop or
- Thyme or
- 1 clove of garlic

Wash the herb well and dip in vinegar. Dry well. Place in a bottle and fill the bottle with olive oil. Close the bottle and store for 10 days out of direct sunlight. Shake the bottle every few days.

Olive Relish

"I am like an olive tree flourishing in the house of God" (Psalm 52:7)

This recipe was recorded by Cato in the first century B.C.E. in his treatise "De Agri Cultura" (About Agriculture)

- 1 cup pitted black olives
- 1 cup pitted green olives
- 4 tbsps red wine vinegar
- 1 heaped tsp crushed coriander seeds (optional)
- 2 tsps finely chopped cilantro
- ½ tsp finely chopped rue or rosemary leaves
- 3 tsps finely chopped mint leaves
- 2 tbsps olive oil

Roughly chop the olives. Place in a bowl, add the remaining ingredients and mix well. Pour over a little olive oil. Serve with Biblical Bread.

Biblical Recipes

Fish

Fish were usually poached or grilled and combined with a sauce.

Fish poached in White Wine

"The fish will be of many kinds" (Ez. 47:10)

- 1 cup white wine
- 1 sliced onion
- salt and pepper
- 1½ cups water
- 2 bay leaves
- 4 fish steaks or fillets

Simmer all ingredients, except the fish, in a wide pan for five minutes. Season to taste. Add the fish and cook till soft, about 5 minutes, depending on size. Remove fish. Serve with one of the following sauces. They can be poured over the fish or served separately.

Tahini (Sesame paste) Sauce

- 1½ cups tahini paste
- 5 tbsps white wine
- 3 crushed garlic cloves
- 3 tbsps chopped parsley

Garnish:
- ½ cup fried blanched almonds, fried onion rings, chopped parsley

Place cooked fish in an oiled oven-proof dish. Mix tahini paste with white wine, garlic and parsley, adding water until a thick sauce is formed. Season to taste and spoon over cooked fish. Bake 15 minutes in a medium-hot oven (325°F, 170°C) until golden-brown and bubbly. Garnish with almonds, onion rings and parsley.

Peter's Herb Sauce

"One of them went out into the fields to gather herbs" (2 Kings 4:39)

- 1 cup leek, chopped
- 5 tbsps olive oil
- 1 cup finely chopped cilantro
- 1 cup finely chopped parsley
- 2 crushed garlic cloves
- 1 tsp ground cumin
- ½ tsp freshly ground black pepper
- 1 tbsp white wine vinegar

Fry the leek in the olive oil until soft. Blend all the ingredients together in a food processor.

Onion and Honey Sauce

"We remember the fish we ate in Egypt...also the onions" (Nu.11:5)

- 2 tbsps olive oil
- 1 sprig rosemary
- ½ cup white wine
- 2 large chopped onions
- 1 bay leaf
- 1 tbsp honey
- salt & freshly-ground black pepper

Cook the onion in the olive oil with the herbs in a covered pan until soft, about 15 minutes. Add the remaining ingredients and cook for a further 10 minutes until thick and most of the liquid has evaporated.

Biblical Recipes

All the salads are based on recipes from "De Re Coquinaria" by Apicius, the first century Roman gourmet.

Beets and Raisin Salad

"Caraway is beaten out with a rod, and cummin with a stick" (Isaiah 28:27)

- 1 large beet
- 2 cups vegetable broth
- ½ tsp ground cumin
- ½ tsp ground coriander
- ½ cup raisins
- 1 cup chopped leek (white part only)
- 3 tbsps olive oil
- 1 tsp flour mixed with ¼ cup water
- ½ tbsp wine vinegar
- Caraway seeds (optional)
- Salt & freshly-ground pepper

Cover the beet with water and cook for 30 mins. Drain. Put vegetable broth, cumin, coriander, raisins, leeks and 2 tbsps. olive oil in a pan, mix well and bring to a boil. Add the beet and cook until soft, about 30 minutes. Remove beet, cool, slice and place in a bowl. Continue cooking the liquid until reduced by half. Add flour mixture and stir till thickened. Add ½ tbsp wine vinegar and 1 tbsp. olive oil and pour over the beet. Sprinkle with caraway seeds, season to taste, and serve at room temperature.

Carrots with cumin

"Does he not ... scatter cumin ?" (Is.28:25)

- 6 medium carrots
- water
- salt
- ¼ cup olive oil
- 1 tbsp honey
- 2 crushed garlic cloves
- ½ tsp ground cumin
- 1 tbsp chopped parsley
- salt & freshly ground pepper

Peel and slice carrots into ¼-inch rounds. Put in a pot with a little water and salt and cook covered for about 10 minutes until tender but still crisp. Mix remaining ingredients and add to the hot carrots. Toss and adjust seasoning to taste. Serve at room temperature.

Fava Bean Salad

"...wheat, barley and beans" (Ez. 4:9)

- 1 cup fava beans
- 4 finely chopped garlic cloves
- 10 finely chopped sprigs of mint
- 1 cup bulghur (cracked wheat)
- 4 tbsps olive oil
- 1 tbsp white wine vinegar
- salt & freshly ground black pepper

Soak the beans in water overnight. Drain, cover with fresh water and cook for ½ hour. Add the bulghur and cook a further 10 minutes. Drain and leave to cool. Add the remaining ingredients and season to taste.

Leek Salad

"We remember the ... leeks, onions and garlic" (Nu. 11:5)

- 2 large leeks
- 3 tbsps olive oil
- 2 tbsps white wine vinegar
- salt & pepper
- 2 tbsps coarsely chopped walnuts

Cut leeks in half lengthways and slice finely. Put in a pan, cover with water, and cook till just tender, about 7 minutes. Mix the oil and vinegar, pour over leeks while still hot and season to taste. Leave to cool. Before serving, sprinkle with nuts.

Bulghur Salad

"A land with wheat and barley, vines and fig trees..." (Deut. 8:8)

- 1 cup bulghur (cracked wheat)
- ½ tsp salt
- 2 tbsps pine nuts
- 2 tbsps blanched almonds
- 1½ cups water
- ¼ cup raisins
- 1 tbsp grape juice
- salt & pepper

Put bulghur, salt, pine nuts, almonds and water in a pan, bring to a boil and simmer gently until tender, about 10 minutes. Add remaining ingredients and season to taste. Serve at room temperature.

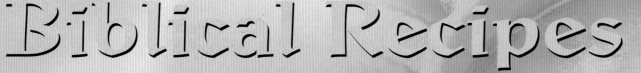

Biblical Recipes

Meat & Poultry

Roast Lamb

A whole lamb was roasted for the Passover meal, as described in Exodus 12.

- 1 shoulder or leg of lamb
- honey or olive oil
- 1 tsp mustard
- 3 finely chopped garlic cloves

Spread the lamb with the honey or olive oil, mustard and garlic. Leave for 1 hour, or longer. Preheat the oven to 350°F (180°C). Place the lamb in a roasting tin and roast for 1 hour.

Martha's Meat Balls

"He who eats meat, eats to the Lord"
(Romans 14:10)

- 1 lb chopped meat
- salt & freshly-ground black pepper to taste
- olive oil for frying

Sauce:
- 1 sliced leek   • ½ cup red wine
- 1 cup concentrated vegetable soup
- ¼ cup sweet wine
- 1 cup chopped celery leaves
- 1 tbsp fresh oregano or ½ tsp dried
- salt & freshly-ground black pepper

Mix the meat with the seasonings and form into small balls. Fry in oil on all sides until golden.

In a large pot, heat 2 tbsps olive oil and add the leek and celery leaves. Sauté until soft. Add the remaining ingredients and cook together for 5 minutes. Gently drop in the meatballs and cook for a further 20 minutes. Season to taste.

Laban's Siniyeh

"You dine on choice lambs and fattened calves" (Amos 6:4)

Base:
- 2 lbs minced lamb
- ½ cup finely chopped onion
- ½ cup finely chopped parsley
- 2 crushed garlic cloves
- ¼ cup olive oil
- ¼ tsp cardamom
- salt & freshly-ground black pepper
- 2 tbsps flour
- ¼ tsp cumin
- ¼ tsp cinnamon

Topping:
- ¾ cup tahini paste
- 2 crushed garlic cloves
- 1 tbsp white wine vinegar
- ½ cup water
- salt & pepper
- 2 tbsps pine nuts

Mix all ingredients for the base, adjust seasonings and put in a round, greased heatproof dish. Bake for 15 minutes at 375°F (190°C).
Mix ingredients for topping and season to taste. Spread over the meat mixture and bake together for 10 minutes. Sprinkle with pine nuts and bake for a further 5 minutes.

Prodigal Son's Veal Stew

- 1½ lb veal shoulder, cut in cubes
- 2 chopped onions
- 2 cloves finely chopped garlic
- freshly ground pepper
- 2 cups beef stock
- 4 sliced young leeks
- freshly-ground black pepper
- 2 tbsp olive oil
- 1 tbsp flour
- 1 tbsp cumin
- 1 tsp salt

Fry veal and onions in oil. Add garlic and flavorings and mix. Sprinkle with flour, stir well and add stock. Cover, bring to the boil and simmer gently for one hour, stirring occasionally. When the meat is tender, add pieces of leek. Simmer for a further 10 minutes and season to taste.

Biblical Recipes

▲ Solomon's Chicken Shishkebab

*"Solomon's daily provisions...
and choice fowl" (1 Kings 4:22-3)*

Marinade:
- 1 clove finely chopped garlic
- 1 tbsp chopped cilantro
- 4 tsp ground cumin
- 2 tsp salt
- 2 tsp freshly-ground black pepper
- 1 tbsp saffron
- 2 tbsp olive oil

Mix all marinade ingredients. Remove chicken from bone and cut into bite-sized pieces. Marinate chicken pieces evenly and leave in refrigerator for 6 hours. Put chicken pieces on wooden skewers and broil for 4-5 minutes on each side.

❖❖ ❖❖❖❖❖❖

The following sauces described by Apicius can be served with 4 partially cooked chicken breasts cut in quarters, or with chicken joints (fried or boiled in a broth). The chicken can be marinated in the sauce for an hour before cooking. Serve with cracked wheat (bulghur).

Mint Sauce

- 1 cup chicken broth
- 1 tbsp wine vinegar
- ¾ cup finely chopped mint leaves
- 2 tbsps finely chopped parsley
- 2 tbsps finely chopped celery
- ½ tsp ground coriander
- ½ cup finely chopped dates
- 1 tbsp honey
- 2 tbsps olive oil
- 1 cup white wine
- salt and pepper

Put the chicken soup, vinegar and herbs in a pan and cook for 5 minutes. Add the remaining ingredients and cook for another 10 minutes until half the liquid has evaporated. Season to taste. Add the chicken breasts or joints and cook together for 5 minutes.

Herb Sauce

- 1 cup chicken broth
- ½ cup finely chopped dill
- ½ cup finely chopped cilantro
- 1 sliced leek
- 3 tbsps olive oil
- salt & pepper to taste
- 1 bottle white wine reduced to 1/3 by boiling

Mix all ingredients except the wine and cook for 10 minutes. Add the chicken breasts and cook together for another 10 minutes. Pour over the grape wine, stir well and serve.

Almond Sauce

- ½ cup chopped dates
- ½ cup chopped almonds
- ½ tsp ground cumin
- ½ tsp rosemary
- 1 tsp wine vinegar
- 1 tsp olive oil
- ½ tsp coriander
- 1 cup chicken stock
- salt & pepper

Mix all the dry ingredients and add vinegar, stock and olive oil. Cook together for 5 minutes, add the chicken and cook for 10 more minutes.

❖❖ ❖❖❖❖❖❖

Stuffed Baby Chickens

4 baby chickens or 1 large chicken

Stuffing:
- 1 cup burghul (cracked wheat)
- 4 cups chicken broth
- 1 finely chopped onion
- 1 tbsp raisins
- 4 tbsps olive oil
- 3 tbsps pine nuts
- salt and freshly-ground black pepper

Soak the cracked wheat in the chicken broth until all liquid is absorbed. Sauté the onion in 2 tbsps of olive oil until transparent. Add the pine nuts and raisins and cook until the nuts are slightly brown. Remove from heat and add to the cracked wheat. Season to taste. Season the birds inside and out and stuff with the cracked wheat mixture. Place in a hot oven for 10 minutes, reduce to medium heat and bake for 40 minutes until golden, basting occasionally with olive oil. Serve the remaining cracked wheat with the chickens.

Biblical Recipes

Sweets

Song of Songs Nut Cakes

"nard and saffron, calamus and cinnamon"
(S. of S. 4:14)

This is an ancient Egyptian recipe from 1600 B.C.E, discovered on an ostracon.

- 1 cup fresh or juicy dried pitted dates or figs
- ¼ -½ cup water
- 1 tsp ground cinnamon
- ¼ tsp ground cardamom
- ½ cup chopped walnuts
- ¾ cup chopped almonds
- honey

In a blender or food processor, mix the dates to a paste with the water. Add the spices, walnuts and ¼ cup almonds and mix well. Form into small balls, coat with honey and roll in remaining almonds.

❖❖ ❖❖❖❖❖ ❖

Sages' Wheat Dessert

"a land with wheat and barley ... pomegranates, olive oil and honey"
(Deut. 8:8)

This is also great as a breakfast cereal

- 1 cup cracked wheat
- 2-3 tbsps honey
- ½ cup coarsely chopped walnuts
- ½ tsp salt
- ¼ cup pomegranate seeds (optional)

Soak the cracked wheat in water for 3 hours. Drain, cover with fresh water and cook for 1 hour. Towards the end of the cooking time, add honey to taste. Drain and cool. Soak nuts in 1 cup water with salt for 3 minutes. Drain, and roast salted nuts in the oven until brown. Cool. Add nuts and pomegranate seeds to the cracked wheat. Can add more honey to taste.

Joanna's Semolina Cake with Almonds

"honey and curds, sheep and cheese from cows' milk" *(2 Sam. 17:29)*

- 1 cup butter
- ½ cup honey
- 1 cup ground almonds
- 2 tbsps yogurt
- ½ cup blanched almonds, halved
- 1 cup milk
- 2 cups semolina

Syrup:
- ⅔ cup honey
- ⅓ cup water
- ½ tsp cinnamon

Grease an 8″ square baking tin.
Place ingredients for the syrup in a pot and bring to a boil. Simmer for 5 minutes.
Heat the butter, milk and honey till boiling and remove from the heat. Add the semolina, almonds and yogurt and mix well. Fold in the blanched almonds. Pour into baking pan and bake at 180°C (350°F) for 30-40 minutes until golden brown. Remove from oven and pour syrup over immediately. Cut into squares and serve warm or cold.

Roman Nut Cake

"a little honey, some spices and myrrh, some pistachio nuts, almonds" (Gen. 43:11)

- 4 ozs ground walnuts • 4 ozs ground hazelnuts
- 4 ozs ground almonds • 3 ozs pitted,dried dates
- 3 ozs dried figs • 6 tbsps honey
- ½ tsp freshly ground black pepper
- 6 ozs sesame seeds

Spread nuts on a baking tray and put under a medium-hot grill for 5 minutes, stirring frequently to prevent burning. Blend the dates and figs in a food processor and add the nuts and pepper. Heat the honey in a pan till foaming and boil for 3 minutes. Add ⅓ to the fruit and nut mixture and blend. Put the sesame seeds in a bowl and stir in the remaining honey. Divide the sesame mixture into two. With wet hands, flatten ½ into a 9" square dish. Spread fruit and nut mixture over the sesame mixture and with wet hands, flatten remaining sesame seeds on top. Leave to set for one hour and with a wet knife, cut into small squares.

Susanna's Cinnamon Pears

"take the following fine spices ... fragrant cinnamon ..." (Rev.18:13)

- 4 medium pears
- 1½ cups red wine
- 3 tbsps honey
- ½ tsp ground cinnamon
- ¼ tsp nutmeg
- ½ tsp cumin
- 1 tsp flour mixed with ¼ cup cold water

Peel, core and quarter the pears. Put wine, honey and spices in a pan and bring to the boil. Add the pears and cook for 15 mins. until soft. Remove pears and put in a dish. Continue boiling until half the liquid has evaporated. Mix flour with water, add to the liquid and stir till thick. Pour over pears and cool.

Roman Melon

"We remember ...in Egypt the...cucumbers, melons"

- ½ melon • ½ water melon
- 1 cup sweet wine • 1 tbsp parsley, chopped
- ½ tsp freshly-ground pepper
- mint to garnish

Peel and dice melon and put in a pot together with the wine and parsley. Boil lightly for 5 minutes and leave to cool. Garnish with mint.

John's Honey-Baked Figs

"...a hundred cakes of figs and a skin of wine" (2 Sam. 16:1)

- ½ lb dried figs
- ⅓ cup chopped walnuts
- 1 cup dry red wine
- ¼ cup clear honey

Make a hole at the stem end of each fig and stuff with walnuts. Place in a 6" casserole. Mix the wine and honey and pour over the figs. Cover and bake for 30 minutes. Serve at room temperature.

Stuffed Dates in Honey

- 20 pitted dates
- ¼ cup honey
- 10 blanched halved almonds or halved walnuts
- salt & freshly-ground black pepper

Stuff each date with half an almond or walnut and dip in salt. Heat the honey gently, and when it starts to foam, drop in the dates. Cook for a short time, without allowing the honey to caramelize. Remove the dates from the honey with a slotted spoon and let cool on baking paper. Sprinkle with black pepper.

Biblical Recipes

How Much Did Food Cost?

One amphora of olive oil = 1 denarius

An ox = 100-200 denarii

A lamb = 4 denarii

A calf = 20 denarii

A cluster of grapes = 1 prutah

A festive meal = 1 silver denarius

One seah of flour = 1 silver denarius

One kor of wheat = 25 silver denarii

A loaf of bread = 1/12 silver denarius

A ram = 8 denarii

One pomegranate = 1 prutah

A small citron = 1 prutah

The talmudic tractate *Pe'ah*, which deals with food to be given to the poor, determined that "ten walnuts, five peaches, two pomegranates, or a single citron" - the equivalent of two good meals - were a proper donation to the poor.

Bibliography

Amar Zohar, "Like Snow in Summer": A Luxury Product in the Land of Israel and Syria. Cathedra Vol. 102, December 2001 (Hebrew).

Amiran, Ruth. The Ancient Pottery of the Land of Israel from the Beginning and until the Destruction of the First Temple. Jerusalem: Bialik Institute and the IEJ, 1971.

Biblesoft: PC Study Bible. Biblesoft Inc., www.Biblesoft.com.

Biven, David. "Matthew 5:13: Saltless Salt?" Jerusalem Perspective Online, July 2002.

Bar Ilan University. The Responsa Project, Version 2.0 (CD-ROM edition of the Hebrew Bible, The Babylonian Talmud, and the Mishna).

Berlin, Andrea M. "What's For Dinner? The Answer is in the Pot." Biblical Archaeological Review, Nov/Dec 1999.

Broshi, Magen. Food of the People of the Land of Israel in the Roman Period. In: Cathedra 43, April 1987, pp. 15-32 (Hebrew)

Clark, Bill. First Christmas Gifts: Gold, Frankincense, and Myrrh. Israel Ministry of Tourism Information Department Press Release, 1991.

Cline, Eric H. Sailing the Wine Dark Sea: International Trade and the Late Bronze Age Aegean. Oxford: B.A.R. International Series 591, 1994.

Cooper, John. Eat and Be Satisfied: a Social History of Jewish Food. Northvale, NJ: Jason Aronson, Inc., 1993.

Crowfoot, Grace M. and Louise Baldensperger. From Cedar to Hyssop: A Study in the Folklore of Plants in Palestine. London: The Sheldon Press, 1932.

Dayagi-Mendeles, Michal. Wine and Beer in Ancient Times. Jerusalem: Israel Museum, 1999

Edelstein, Gershon and Shimon Gibson. "Ancient Jerusalem's Rural Food Basket." Biblical Archaeological Review, Vol VIII No. 4 July/Aug 1982, pp 46-54.

Edwards, John. The Roman Cookery of Apicius. London: Random House, 1993.

Encyclopedia Judaica, CD Rom Edition. Judaica Multimedia, text: Keter Publishing House.

Eretz Israel Museum, The Corn Spirit, Tel Aviv, 2002.

Felix, Yehuda. Nature and Man in the Bible. London: Soncino Press, 1981.

Finkelstein, Israel and Neil Asher Silberman. The Bibl Unearthed. New York: The Free Press, 2000.

Forbes, R.J. Studies in Ancient Technology Vol 5. Leider Netherlands: EK Brill, 1995.

Frankel, Raphael. Wine and Oil Production in Ancier Israel and other Mediterranean Countries. Sheffield Sheffield Academic, 1999.

Golan Archaeological Museum, Katzrin Park. *Talmu Kelim:* The Literal and Homiletic in the Daily Life at th Time of the Talmud (Hebrew).

Gonen, Rivka. Grain: The Dagon Collection. Jerusalem Shikmona Publishing Co, 1979

Goor, Asaph and Max Nurock, Fruits of the Holy Lanc Jerusalem, London, NY: Israel Universities Press, 196£

Goor, Asaph, The History of the Rose in the Holy Lanc Pittsburgh, PA: Hunt Botanical Library. Carnegie Mello University, 1970.

Hareuveni, Nogah. Nature in Our Biblical Heritag Kiryat Ono: Neot Kedumim, 1980.

Horwitz, L.K., Tchernove, E., et. al. "Animal Domesticatio in the Southern Levant." Paleorient, Vol. 25/2, 1999, pp 63-80.

Josephus, F. Jewish Antiquities, Heinemann, 1981.

Josephus, F. The Jewish War, Penguin, 1981.

Mazar, Amichai. Archaeology of the Land of the Bible New York: Doubleday, 1990.

McGovern, Pat, and Stuart J. Flemming, eds. Origins an Ancient History of Wine. Luxembourg: Gordon an Breach, 1995.

McMinley, Judith. "Gendering Wisdom the Host: Biblica Invitations to Eat and Drink." Journal for the Study o the Old Testament. Supplement Series 216. ed J. Chery Exum. Sheffield, England: Sheffield Academic Pres: 1996.

Myers, Allen C., ed. The Eerdmans Bible Dictionar Grand Rapids, Mich.: Eerdmans Publishing Compan 1987.

Rabinowitz, Louis I. Torah and Flora. NY: Sanhedri Press, 1977.

Safrai, Shmuel. The Time of the Second Temple and th Period of the Mishna. Israel Ministry of Education, 197 (Hebrew).

Shapiro, Samantha M. "Negotiations With Appetite." The Jerusalem Report, Aug. 12, 2002

Tsukerman, S., "A New Way to Prepare Cheese", *Teva Vaaretz*, Volume 8, 1966, p. 227-228 (Hebrew).

Wagner, Clarence. Everyday Life in Bible Times; Farming in the Bible Part 4. Daily Bread. The Bridges for Peace Website: Bridgesforpeace.com

Wagner, Clarence. Everyday Life in Bible Times; Farming in the Bible Part 5. Livestock. The Bridges for Peace Website: Bridgesforpeace.com

Walsh, Carey Ellen. The Fruit of the Vine: Viniculture in Ancient Israel. Harvard Semitic Museum Publications, Lawrence E, Stager, Gen. Ed. Wiboba Lake, Ind.: Eisenbrauns Press, 2000

Zohary, Michael. Plants of the Bible. Cambridge: Cambridge Univ. Press, 1982.

What Is the Talmud?

As noted in the Foreword, the Talmud is a collection of commentaries on the Bible, set down in writing in the early centuries after the time of Jesus. The Talmud has two parts: The Mishna, which was compiled in about 200 CE in the city of Sepphoris in the Galilee, and the Gemara, commentaries on the Mishna based on discussions and debates that took place in rabbinic academies. The Gemara has two versions, both of which include the text of the Mishna: it appears as the Jerusalem Talmud, composed in the Land of Israel, and the Babylonian Talmud, composed later than the Jerusalem Talmud (around 500 CE), by rabbis who lived outside of the Land of Israel. By looking very closely at each verse - and very often each word - of the Bible, rabbis and sages were able to compose a body of rules and customs that would help people live as a community in a new reality, after the Temple was destroyed.

Both editions of the Talmud relate to everyday life, with the Jerusalem Talmud, though less extensive than the Babylonian Talmud, focusing on life in the Holy Land, including details about agriculture, home life, food and cooking, among many other subjects. Because in many instances the Talmud can enlighten us about these same subjects in the New Testament, it has become an increasingly important source of study for Christians, both scholars and lay people.

Both the Talmud and the Mishna are composed of tractates, or treatments of subjects. Among the many tractates that provided valuable background information for our discussion of foods and customs in ancient times were: Kiddushin, which deals with matrimonial matters, Shabbat, outlining aspects of Sabbath observance, Ketuboth, which discusses the rights and obligations of the Jewish marriage contract, and Bikkurim, regarding the laws of the First Fruits.

Index